JUDICIAL JEOPARDY

Other Books By
Richard Neely

How Courts Govern America
Why Courts Don't Work
The Divorce Decision

JUDICIAL JEOPARDY

When Business Collides with the Courts

RICHARD NEELY

Addison-Wesley Publishing Company, Inc.

Reading, Massachusetts   Menlo Park, California
Don Mills, Ontario   Wokingham, England
Amsterdam   Sydney   Singapore   Tokyo
Madrid   Bogota   Santiago   San Juan

Library of Congress Cataloging-in-Publication Data

Neely, Richard, 1941–
  Judicial jeopardy.

  Includes bibliographical references.
  1. Courts — United States.   2. Judicial process —
United States.   3. Political questions and judicial
power — United States.   4. Industry and state — United
States.   I. Title.
KF8700.N44   1986   347.73'1   86-7945
ISBN 0-201-05736-0   347.3071

Cover design by Rogalski Associates, Inc.
Text design by Carson Designs
Set in 11 point Palatino by Compset, Inc., Beverly, MA
ABCDEFGHIJ-DO-89876
First printing, October 1986

For my friend, the late J. Harper Meredith, Chief Judge of the Circuit Court of Marion County, West Virginia, from 1946 to 1984. A man of honor, integrity, and intelligence who brought peace to our valley for almost forty years.

A good deal of the wisdom of life is apt to appear foolishness to a narrow logic. We urge our horse down hill and yet put the brake on the wheel — clearly a contradictory process to a logic too proud to learn from experience. But a genuinely scientific logic would see in this humble illustration a symbol of that measured straining in opposite directions which is the essence of that homely wisdom which makes life livable.

Morris R. Cohen

Contents

Introduction

In 1960 the Committee to Defend Martin Luther King and the Struggle for Freedom in the South bought a full-page advertisement in *The New York Times* in which the committee made patently untrue allegations about the conduct of the Montgomery police department during civil rights protests. Among the false statements in the advertisement was one that said: "In Montgomery, Alabama, after students sang 'My Country 'Tis of Thee' on the State Capitol steps, their leaders were expelled from school, and truckloads of police armed with shotguns and tear-gas ringed the Alabama State College Campus." L. B. Sullivan, one of three elected commissioners of the City of Montgomery, Alabama, and the supervisor of that city's police department, sued *The New York Times* and the committee for libel. The Alabama courts found the statements both false and libelous and awarded Commissioner Sullivan $500,000 in damages.

The New York Times appealed to the Supreme Court of the United States, and in March 1964 the Supreme Court rendered its opinion in *New York Times v. Sullivan* — probably the most important decision on freedom of speech in U.S. history. The Supreme Court held that the first amendment to the U.S. Constitution precludes state court libel judgments against newspapers for publishing false statements about public officials unless a newspaper either knows at the time of publication that the statements are false or behaves with reckless disregard of the truth.

We usually think of *New York Times v. Sullivan* as a case about our constitutional right to free expression, but it is also an important business case. *Sullivan* wiped out in one stroke the only "product liability" hazard that threatens the media industry. Furthermore, the Supreme Court preempted state libel law, and in its place imposed a uniform national standard of liability with a very high threshold. *Sullivan* opened up virtually unlimited profit-making opportunities for newspapers, magazines, and broadcasters. And to make the profit picture better, logical extensions of the *Sullivan* doctrine have led to special procedural rules in libel cases — such as the liberal granting of summary judgments — that protect the media from bankrupting legal fees as well as from bankrupting final judgments.

Once *Sullivan* is viewed as a business case rather than a free speech case, its irony becomes obvious. During the last twenty-six years, as the Supreme Court was nationalizing our libel law and providing progressively greater protection for the media, state courts were racing one another to expand the tort liability of the United States' smokestack and service industries without any efforts whatsoever by the U.S. Supreme Court to establish uniform national standards. Yet there is no reason to believe that newspapers and broadcasters are less meretricious than car manufacturers, tobacco companies, or doctors. The media regularly drum up scandals from the basest motives and injure innocent people. Even the great journalism schools reluctantly admit that the media are in the entertainment business and not the information business.[1]

The decision to treat the media differently from all other industries was exclusively a political decision. Consequently, the lesson to be learned from *New York Times v. Sullivan* is that business has political problems in the courts and not narrow legal problems. *Sullivan* and later cases expanding its doctrine simply reflect the Supreme Court's political conclusion that making the media pay for the injuries they cause would lead to such self-censorship that government by free discussion would be in jeopardy.

Judges have no illusions about either the integrity or the motives of the media, but judges understand that the free flow of information has a higher social priority than the right of individuals

---

[1]N. Postman, *Amusing Ourselves to Death* (New York: Viking Press, 1985).

to security in their reputations. If courts impose liability on the media for negligent libel, the media will simply reject serious political discussion and concentrate exclusively on noncontroversial entertainment. CBS's "Sixty Minutes" would stop doing hard-hitting stories about doctors involved in welfare fraud and replace them with stories about 106-year-olds who make their own molasses from sorghum.

Every year the courts are creating new types of liability that threaten business, yet as the history of the media since *Sullivan* demonstrates, courts can eliminate forms of business liability as easily as they can create them. Furthermore, *Sullivan* also demonstrates that it is not inevitable that business be subjected to the parochial laws of the fifty separate states. The federal courts can nationalize the law of products liability as easily as they nationalized the law of libel!

Whether the courts will expand or restrict liability, then, is largely a political decision. Neither the law concerning free speech for newspapers and broadcasters enunciated in *Sullivan* nor today's law of products liability flows ineluctably from constitutional principles, older case law, or the English common law. England, unlike the United States, restricts the media's profit-making opportunities through draconian libel laws, but England also makes it hard for an injured consumer to win damages against a manufacturer.

Landmark court decisions concerning business are predicated not on legal principles but rather on social, political, and economic principles that instruct judges' understandings of the public good. The policy behind modern product liability law, for example, is that many of society's risks can be spread through universal insurance purchased by business and paid for by consumers through higher prices. If, therefore, business wants to restrict its liability in specific areas, business must show the courts compelling social, political, and economic reasons for such restrictions.

Indeed, there are numerous instances where such showings can be made. Experience has taught us that the risk-spreading, insurance model implicit in product liability law is not *universally* applicable. For example, widespread vaccination has reduced the risks of most of the dreaded diseases of yesteryear such as diphtheria, measles, German measles (rubella), mumps, hepatitis B., and influenza — to mention just a few — to insignificant levels. But in the 1980s state courts handed down several six-figure judgments against the manufacturers of the Sabin polio vaccine because the vaccine induced cases of polio. Those of us who remember when polio presented an annual terror understand that the vaccine's risk of less than one in a million of inducing polio in innoculees is far better than 15,000 serious cases a year.

Yet tort liability currently jeopardizes universal vaccination, and thoughtful judges are listening carefully to political arguments that justify special liability rules for pharmaceutical companies in vaccine-related cases. According to the Harvard Medical School, rates of immunization are as low as 60 percent in some communities — particularly poor communities where children are at high risk. At the same time, expensive insurance premiums are driving the major drug companies out of the vaccine business, and if the remaining companies raise their prices to cover escalating insurance costs, the likelihood is that fewer children will be vaccinated. People have little incentive to pay for immunization when a disease has been virtually eradicated, but if we fail to maintain high levels of immunization, once-dreaded diseases will reappear in perhaps even more virulent forms.

Considerations such as how liability affects media self-censorship or how high insurance costs jeopardize universal immunization are "political" in the highest sense of the word. It is in that sense, then, that I point out that business has political problems and not legal problems in court. Contrary to popular belief, legal rules seldom proceed exclusively from some body of abstract "legal" principles; rather, legal rules usually proceed from courts' understanding (or misunderstanding) of applicable social, political, and economic principles.

Improving business' track record in the courts involves placing the courts in a much broader social, political, and economic context than business management usually imagines. It is from an analysis of this broader context that business will develop improved political approaches to what are essentially political problems. Yet not all political problems come with obvious labels attached to them. The social dynamics that create a bad climate for business in the courts often involve obscure series of causes and effects that make it difficult to piece together what has happened.

For example, from 1967 to 1977 there was a shortage of lawyers. Demand resulted in high starting salaries in law firms, and students responded by applying to law schools in greater numbers. Existing law schools expanded enrollment, and new schools were built. The number of practicing lawyers in the United States increased from 265,823 in 1967 to 653,686 in 1985 — a 146 percent increase in eighteen years. By 1985, however, the market for lawyers was glutted. Yet U.S. law schools continue to turn out 35,000 lawyers a year in the face of a severe decline in qualified applicants because law schools have debts to repay, tenured faculty to employ, and community pressure to offer places to local students.

Surplus lawyers, however, are not a passive commodity like surplus grain or cheese; lawyers vindicate Say's law that supply creates its own demand. When lawyers are climbing over one another to find work, their answer to unemployment is to *create* work by encouraging people to sue one another. It is no accident that the recent liberalization of ethical rules so that lawyers can now advertise coincided with the lawyer glut. As the client market gets tighter, many lawyers are turning to television to flog their services and increase their market shares. How much the courts cost business, therefore, both in terms of damage awards and legal fees, is directly related to the price, availability, and quality of the lawyers who sue them. When the qualifications of applicants to law schools decline, more low-quality lawyers are produced. These low-quality lawyers lack the ability to enter demanding fields like tax law or administrative law where there are available jobs and inevitably turn their energies to ambulance chasing. As a result, business suffers from an increase in nuisance suits.

Furthermore, the lawyer surplus not only affects the number of times that business is dragged into court, but it also affects the number of occasions on which plaintiffs can invite courts to change the law in a way unfavorable to business. Because courts formulate social policy only in the context of the cases brought to them, an increase in the number of cases brought to court expands courts' power relative to other political policy-makers, like legislatures, administrative agencies, and executives.

Business management tends to look on their court-related problems in legal terms, but the problems that surplus lawyers create must be viewed in political terms. Higher bar admission standards, a reduction in the size of law school classes, and court-imposed penalties against lawyers who file frivolous suits are all possible political responses to this political problem.

Surplus lawyers are simply one illustration of the proposition that the results that business gets in court depend on a host of factors far removed from the courts themselves. To take another example, both the design of a law firm and the corresponding corporate structure of a client may create counterproductive approaches to litigation. Specifically, corporate managers are fiduciaries who feel most comfortable when they pay their lawyers by the hour. Big defense law firms respond to their clients' accounting requirements by adopting case management systems that allow them to "build a file" that creates a paper trail to justify their bills.

But business defendants can often dispose of lawsuits most cheaply by making low but immediate offers to impecunious plaintiffs who, for entirely subjective reasons, are willing to give an unreasonably large discount to defendants for quick cash. In this circumstance the client's interest and the law firm's interest are diametrically opposed; without months or years of depositions, interrogatories, and pretrial motions the law firm cannot build a file to justify a large fee, and large fees are necessary to sustain the overhead of large firms. Clients, then, can find themselves engaged in potentially disastrous, all-or-nothing litigation simply because their lawyers are in the litigation business and not the cheap settlement business.

Formulating the right questions to solve any business problem is usually more difficult than coming up with the correct answers. More of the right questions can be formulated by looking at the total social system in which courts operate than by simply looking at a series of individual, unrelated cases. In fact, looking at the total system one sees that the lawsuit likely to do any particular business the most damage is another business' lawsuit! Courts not only decide cases, but in the course of deciding cases throw off interpretations of the law — a by-product that affects all businesses alike.

In their lawmaking function courts are like legislatures; through particular cases they articulate new legal rules or change old ones, and these new or changed rules apply with equal force whether Congress or a state legislature enacts them. When, for example, the Supreme Court of the United States decides a case between the owner of a $500,000 rural apartment complex in Montana and the Internal Revenue Service about allowable rates of depreciation, the legal conclusions that emerge in the court's opinion in that uninspiring case become law for the owners of billions of dollars of real estate in New York!

For reasons that have to do with institutions outside the courts — particularly the dynamics of legislatures and administrative agencies — the courts will be even more powerful ten years from now than they are today. Over the last twenty years there has been a decisive shift in the center of political power in the direction of the courts, and there is no reason for this trend to abate. Courts, then, must be perceived for what they are — both lawmakers and administrators — and business must gear itself up to be as successful in the court political forum as it is in Congress, the state legislatures, or the administrative agencies.

This book is devoted to three major subjects: an explanation of the mechanics of how courts operate; an exploration of how influences outside the courts are forcing judges to take a progressively more prominent governing role; and finally, a way of approaching government by judiciary that is likely to improve business' overall in-court performance, at least at the margin. I hope this book will allow executives, corporate lawyers, public affairs officers, and all others who read it to ask new and strategic legal questions and to act accordingly.

In the writing of this book I have had the help and advice of many people. At each stage in the preparation of the manuscript I have shared the ideas and conclusions with my friends in business and at the bar around the country to ensure that my generalized observations and prescriptions are not so generalized as to be misleading in specific cases. I am grateful for the advice and counsel that I have received.

My preeminent thanks, however, go to my own staff, particularly my administrative assistant, Betty Barnsgrove Price. Betty generally supervised the preparation of the manuscript, typed and retyped the chapters, and also read everything carefully to ensure that what was written was intelligible to an interested lay person. Special thanks are also in order to Lea Ann Van Meter who typed late into the night to get my manuscripts out on time. My brilliant law clerks, Nathaniel D. Chapman and Rolin Bissell, worked with me on the substance and language of the manuscript and mobilized their friends and associates around the country to check the accuracy of our observations.

The editors, Robin Manna and George Gibson, have also made valuable contributions to the concept, wording, structure, and even the content of the book, and finally, my friend, Professor Cecil Y. Lang of the University of Virginia, did his usual excellent editing job to ensure that many lawyerisms were eliminated and that my usage and grammar were up to acceptable standards of literacy (for a lawyer).

Chapter 1

The Politics
of Courts

Americans *love democracy but hate the politicians who make* democracy work. Ever since the early years of the Republic we have searched persistently for some scheme to liberate government from politics and politicians. George Washington's warnings about the dangers of political parties, our extensive civil service system, the populist devices of referendum and initiative, and the recently enacted limits on campaign spending are examples of attempts either to separate government from politicians or to reduce the influence certain groups have over politicians. In such an atmosphere it follows logically that the politicians who will have the most power are the ones who best disguise the fact that they are politicians at all. And judges are masters of disguise.

Although the media report court rulings in the same dispassionate tones that they report baseball scores, there is almost no media attention to the why or how of court decisions. The secret of the courts' low media profile is that both courts as institutions and judges as individuals are excruciatingly boring. Big-time media companies make money in the entertainment, not the information, business. Daily papers and TV networks cannot devote valuable space or time to courts — a subject that evokes only yawns from most readers or viewers. Jesse Jackson's hopeless bid for the presidency

in 1984 received incalculably more media attention than the combined courts in the United States had received in the preceding four
years, simply because Jesse Jackson is interesting but not powerful
while courts are powerful but not interesting.

Judges capitalize on being boring and design their professional
demeanor to accentuate their dullness. Judges never attack anyone
publicly or even defend themselves from the attacks of others; they
never talk to the press about public issues; and they try to live sober,
plodding, noncontroversial personal lives. The result is that few
businessmen can name more than four out of nine U.S. Supreme
Court justices, even though next to the president they are collectively the most powerful men and woman in the United States. The
lower federal courts and the state courts also exercise enormous
power, yet the judges of these courts are almost completely
anonymous.

Ironically, it seldom crosses anyone's mind that many judges
are worn and retreaded politicians — that's how they got to be
judges in the first place. At the federal level, where judges are appointed for life by the president with the advice and consent of the
Senate, a majority have had prior political experience. As often as
not, federal judgeships are given as consolation prizes to those who
have come up short in big-time, elected politics. Many unsuccessful
candidates for governor, Congress, or the Senate are now sitting
beneath the U.S. eagle in black robes, but if they are on the right
courts, they are probably making more law than the representatives
and senators who once-upon-a-time beat them at the polls. Indeed,
the great Earl Warren, a former governor of California, never as-
pired during his political career to be chief justice of the United
States; he wanted to be president.

Twenty-two states elect all their state court judges at regular,
contested elections, and the other twenty-eight states have selection
systems that also guarantee that politicians will become judges. Illinois and Pennsylvania, for example, initially elect their state
judges on a nonpartisan ballot and then have retention elections at
regular intervals where the voter is asked only whether he wishes
to retain a sitting judge. In other states, such as Colorado and Ne-

braska, judges are first appointed and then run in retention elections. In Connecticut and Massachusetts, judges are appointed to serve until mandatory retirement, and in Virginia, Rhode Island, and South Carolina judges are elected by the legislature. Politicians are more skilled than others at winning elections — partisan, nonpartisan, or legislative — and where judges are appointed, the appointments are made by politicians who often appoint other politicians to whom they are indebted.

In my own case, I entered politics to become a United States senator, not a state supreme court judge. It was only after spending six months of 1971 in an exploratory campaign for the U.S. Senate against a fourteen-year incumbent that I realized I had better settle for a seat on West Virginia's highest state court. Running for judge was an easy race for a politician — lawyers without statewide political exposure were my only competition. I won handily in spite of the fact that I was only thirty-one years old and had less notion about what judges did than a one-gallused justice of the peace assigned to night court. But except for my extreme youth, my case is typical. In the normal course of things in this country, prior government service and extensive involvement in elected politics are more likely to lead to a judgeship than extraordinary ability as either a practicing lawyer or a law professor.

Our time-honored path to the judiciary explains, in large part, why U.S. judges — unlike their English or French counterparts — are not reluctant lawmakers. With the exception of a few tired political hacks who take judgeships for early retirement, most judges — and particularly the highest-level judges — welcome opportunities to make their marks on the world. It was to influence political life, after all, that prompted them to choose politics as a career in the first place. The proposition that judges have no agendas — that they sit passively and decide only those issues brought to them by litigants — is pure fantasy. During thirteen years of attending national judicial meetings I have found few judges without agendas. Even more, although this is against the canons of judicial ethics, I know judges who telephone lawyers to encourage them to bring certain types of cases before their courts.

Unlike executives, legislators, or administrators, it is unseemly, however, for judges to appear to be pursuing agendas independent of the cases brought to them. Courts make a significant portion of the law that governs everyday life, but this lawmaking process proceeds only in the context of contested issues brought to the courts by contending litigants. Thus the mechanics of the process contributes to the nonpolitical illusion that is the foundation of judicial power because it always appears that policy-making has been forced on the courts rather than invited by them. Furthermore, the pedestrian nature of most lawsuits combined with the obscurity and complexity of the language used in legal opinions sustains a level of boredom guaranteed to ward away news-seeking journalists.

The total judicial lawmaking process is fairly complicated, but the broad outline is easy enough to explain. The power of the courts to make law comes from two sources: (1) the authority of courts to modify a centuries-old body of law that was originally made in England by the courts themselves called "common law" and (2) the authority of courts to interpret the federal and state constitutions and all the statutes passed by Congress and state legislatures.

Understanding court-made decisional law, or common law, requires a brief excursion into history. The U.S. legal system was inherited from England. In medieval England the judges were officers of the king, and in the three centuries after the Norman conquest of 1066, judges were sent from the king's court to all the outlying areas of England to establish law. In fact, the English word *court*, which is used to denote both the bureaucracy surrounding a king and a judicial tribunal, is lingering evidence that in the early days of the English legal system kings were considered the ultimate judges and judges were considered surrogate kings with extensive administrative and lawmaking powers.

The law that royal judges established came to be called the common law because it was an attempt by royal agents representing the central authority to unify all the different parts of England —

which had previously enjoyed local law and custom — under one set of laws. Thus the word *common* in the context of law does not mean *vulgar* but rather *uniform*. For many centuries in early English history the courts made almost all the law. The English parliament was a late bloomer in the lawmaking business, and by the fifteenth century when Parliament was strong enough to exert a commanding influence over the total legal structure, courts had already made most of the law that anyone wanted or needed.

Thus in the seventeenth century, when parliaments became so hyperactive and turf-conscious that they caused a civil war, it was still generally accepted that courts could and should make law in areas that Parliament chose not to regulate. From the fifteenth century on, in fact, parliaments often passed statutes changing court-made rules or regulating things that courts had left free from regulation. Under the system we inherited, then, it was accepted that when Parliament decided to act, Parliament's pronouncements would override whatever court-made, decisional law had previously been in place. But Parliament acted rarely in such areas of private law as torts,[1] contracts, trusts, estates, and even land tenure. Accordingly, these matters have to this day been left largely to the regulation of the courts, which have developed an extensive body of decisional law on each subject.

After the American Revolution, the courts continued to operate much as they had before the Revolution, and today's American law has evolved from eighteenth-century English law. The U.S. system of decisional lawmaking is now 200 years old. Part of the reason that it has retained such vitality is that Congress and state legislatures have neither the time nor the will to address the nits and lice of private law. The dramatic difference in the proportion of legislatively enacted statutory law to court-made decisional law among the fifty states is eloquent testimony that legislatures let courts make

---

[1]Basically, a tort is a civil wrong for which money damages can be awarded. Torts can be divided into two classes: intentional and negligent. An intentional tort would be a deliberate, unjustified firing of a tenured employee, while a negligent tort would be driving over the speed limit as a result of which someone or some property is injured.

law because they can't or won't do it themselves. In the industrial states like New York, California, and Illinois there are far more statutes governing private law matters like torts or contracts than there are in the rural states like Virginia, Vermont, and Iowa. Unsurprisingly, the industrial states have full-time state legislatures, while the rural states have part-time state legislatures that meet only sixty or ninety days a year. Even in legislatures, work tends to expand to fill the time allotted to do it.

The biggest areas of the law that are governed primarily by court decisions are contracts and torts. Indeed, every state has some statutes that regulate narrow areas of contract or tort law, but these statutes are in addition to, or simply amplify, an exhaustive body of decisional law that comprises the bulk of contract and tort rules. It is decisional law, for example, that determines such questions as the proper measure of damages in most lawsuits, the types of defenses that can be raised against certain contract and tort claims, and the level of evidence that a plaintiff must introduce before a case may be submitted to a jury.

Products liability is a good example of a body of law that has evolved through the courts' authority to change their own decisional rules. Products liability law is an extension of centuries-old tort law, but in the last twenty-five years the courts have so modified traditional tort principles as they apply to products that today's law bears almost no resemblance to what the law looked like in 1960. Products liability law grew over the past twenty-five years in response to a host of considerations — including the increased danger of modern society, the increasing sophistication of our insurance industry, changes in the social consensus on the proper distribution of wealth, and individuals' greater willingness to shift their own burdens to others by seeking redress in the courts. Twenty-five years ago, in order to recover for any personal injury it was necessary to prove that the party who caused the injury was negligent. Now, under the modern doctrine of products liability, an injured person need show only that he was injured and that the injury was the result of a defect in a product — the manufacturer's negligence is simply presumed.

The process by which the law of products liability emerged is instructive for our purposes because it is an example of how judges make law based on evaluations of appropriate social policy. Products liability law actually started in the law schools, where professors wrote law review articles discussing opportunities to use tort law as a vehicle for spreading risk of serious injury through society-wide insurance coverage. It was argued that if manufacturers and distributors were required to pay for all injuries that resulted from defective products, two useful things would occur: First, manufacturers and distributors would purchase insurance to protect themselves, which would indirectly protect injured victims; and second, the insurance companies would demand safer products. The new products liability law has on occasion caused injustice and hardship because its burden has often fallen on companies that could not procure insurance; but taken as a whole the new laws have basically achieved the social purposes that their academic proponents claimed they would achieve. To be convinced, the unbeliever need only travel in Britain or France and observe the significantly higher level of danger in those societies.

Although products liability law is a major issue that affects a large constituency of manufacturers and consumers, court decisions that regulate liability in most other areas affect very few people at any particular time. The agendas of legislatures are more crowded today than they were in fifteenth-century England, and before a legislature will act there must be some political pressure for it to do so. But what political constituency cares about exceptions to the general rule that contracts in writing can be changed only by other contracts in writing? Who is passionately committed politically to modernizing the law of wills? In matters such as these, the courts not only have the time and interest necessary to update the law intelligently, but they also have the necessary expertise.

The other major power of courts — namely, their power to interpret the state and federal constitutions and statutes — amplifies the courts' power to tinker at decisional law. Everyone knows that the U.S. Supreme Court makes law by interpreting the U.S. Constitution; integration, abortion, and the reapportionment of state legislatures on the basis of one man/one vote are well-known and far-reaching examples of judicial policymaking grounded on constitutional interpretation. Another is the revolution in the past twenty years in criminal law based on judicial interpretations of different clauses in the Bill of Rights. In addition, federal courts have used the due process clause of the U.S. Constitution to rewrite the law of landlord and tenant, to limit the ability of creditors to attach personal property to satisfy debts, and to circumscribe the power of governments to cut off welfare and other benefits payments.

Instances of court-made law based on interpretations of simple statutes are more obscure. A paradigm of such lawmaking occurs in the field of antitrust, where the pivotal statutes are the Sherman Act and the Clayton Act, both of which are comparatively short and extremely vague. Since the turn of the century it has been the courts that have poured content into antitrust law. And although court modifications of earlier court interpretations of these statutes have come fast and furiously, legislative modifications of the antitrust statutes have been few in number. For example, until 1945 it was not a violation of the antitrust laws for a company to obtain a monopoly in a particular line of commerce if it did so without engaging in predatory behavior and exclusively through superior products, lower prices, and natural growth. Yet in 1945 the Second Circuit court of appeals did an abrupt about-face and said, under the very same statutes that had once permitted monopolies achieved through superior performance, that *all* monopolies, even those acquired through hard work, innovation, and efficiency, were illegal.[2]

---

[2]In the celebrated case *United States v. Aluminum Co. of America (Alcoa)*, 148 F.2d 416 (2nd Cir. 1945), the court changed the focus of antitrust law from an examination of a firm's predatory market practices (in Alcoa's case none could be found), to an inquiry into a firm's market dominance. Indeed Alcoa controlled 90 percent of the domestic "virgin aluminum ingot" market, but to hold that Alcoa had violated section 2 of the Sherman Act without finding that it had engaged in abusive conduct was tantamount to holding that "big is bad."

Because law is partially policymaking and partially a science, courts operate on some combination of what can be called imprecisely political principles on the one hand and scientific principles on the other hand.[3] Different courts, however, operate on different mixes of political and scientific principles. The courts that come closest to resembling a law professor's ideal of principled decision-makers are the trial courts. Because appellate courts demand that trial courts follow appellate court precedent, trial courts have the highest likelihood among all the courts of following the existing law and doing what everyone expects.

Both federal and state intermediate appellate courts tend to be a little more daring in venturing into policy. The Supreme Court of the United States and the highest courts of the fifty states, however, are like so many loose cannons sliding around the legal deck. The ever-growing lawyer population and the multiplicity of lawsuits that those lawyers create overcome whatever obstacles the rules against soliciting cases present to judges who want to rewrite the law. With more than 12 million lawsuits filed every year in the United States, a judge can be sure that every issue that interests him or her will eventually arrive in his or her court. Consequently, the number and variety of cases brought by today's enormous lawyer population create a hazard to business from the courts that is qualitatively different from anything business has faced in the past. In fact, for reasons that I shall discuss in Chapters 3, 4, and 5, the

---

[3]Ever since the twelfth century when the first great law schools emerged in Europe, law professors have attempted to reduce the ad hoc political decisions of judges to a set of principles that will control judges and give society some sort of predictable "rule of law." The law professors have been more successful in the United States than anywhere else: Our court system is the envy of the entire world, and the stability that our courts provide is one of the reasons that every foreigner with money wants to invest here. Law professors and their students who edit the law reviews are extremely important to the integrity of the courts; they are to judges what *The New York Times* and *The Washington Post* are to politicians — the repository of public opinion. But although public opinion influences judges, it does not control judges any more than public opinion controls other politicians.

United States is undergoing a major legal/political revolution that is shifting progressively more political power toward the judiciary.

From the point of view of business, all lawsuits can be divided into two broad categories: (1) lawsuits that may involve considerable money but that present no new legal issues and do not offer judges an invitation to change existing law, and (2) lawsuits that present new issues and that have a precedent-shattering potential. The first category, ordinary lawsuits, includes the overwhelming majority of all cases in court. Ordinary disputes usually center in factual questions such as whether the defendant was driving recklessly or whether the parties intended the acceptance of a certain sum of money to be a compromise of some disputed claim. In ordinary, category (1) lawsuits, the only cases that are interesting are our own. The primary difference between ordinary lawsuits and precedent-shattering lawsuits is that ordinary lawsuits are bad news only for the business that loses the case, while precedent-shattering lawsuits may be bad news for all of business.

For example, in which lawsuit should Ford Motor Company be more interested: (1) a personal injury suit against Ford itself for $200,000 based on a crash occasioned by a defective wheel on a Ford Escort or (2) a suit against General Motors for $200,000 based on the theory that the plaintiff was injured only because the Chevrolet he was driving was not equipped with inflatable airbags? The law governing defective wheels is pretty well settled, but so far no court has said that a car without airbags is defective simply because airbags would have made the car safer. Ford, therefore, if it has an ounce of sense, should be far more concerned about what happens to General Motors in the airbag case than it is about whether it loses $200,000 in its own defective wheel case.

Airbag litigation is an interesting example of how courts can be used to circumvent the political process. All over the United States at this very moment lawyers for plaintiffs are suing car manufacturers on the theory that their clients were hurt because the cars they were driving didn't have inflatable, protective airbags. The plaintiffs' lawyers argue that airbags cost only about $500 to install and that because safety research demonstrates that a person's likelihood of severe injury in a car equipped with airbags is significantly reduced, the carmakers produce a defective product every time they sell a car not equipped with airbags.

The airbag lawsuits invite courts to nullify in one stroke years of lobbying on the part of car producers who have successfully fought compulsory airbags in the political process. Not surprisingly, there have been money and power on both sides of the airbag issue in the political process because the insurance industry has a compelling interest in automobile safety and would like to see airbags become part of a car's standard equipment.[4] Consequently, the carmakers have not been the only organized voice to be heard on the subject. If the carmakers are correct that airbags may add between $500 to $1,500 to the price of a new car, principles of elasticity of demand indicate that new car sales will fall dramatically if airbags become compulsory. This affects not only stockholders' profits, but employment in the auto plants, the financial health of subcontractors and suppliers, the viability of local dealers, and the prosperity of all areas that depend on the auto industry for their economic welfare. All of these considerations inform and influence the judgment of legislators and administrators, but there is no requirement that a court take them into consideration in a specific airbag case. In poli-

---

[4]Three technologies have been proven to mitigate the severity of automobile crash injuries. Manual lap and shoulder belts, if worn, can prevent about 40 percent of fatal injuries and 50 percent of moderate to critical injuries. Automatic belts, which fasten around the occupants of a car when the car door is closed, are slightly less effective than manual belts. Air cushion (airbag) systems, which operate electronically or mechanically during a crash, are designed to deploy only in front and front-angle crashes. They reduce the overall risk of fatality by about 30 percent and the risk of moderate to critical injury by 35 percent. When airbags and lap and shoulder belts are combined, they reduce fatality risk by 50 percent and injury risk by 55 percent. See J. D. Graham, Secretary Dole and the Future of Automobile Airbags, *The Brookings Review* (Summer 1985). Airbags, however, invite vandalism: A nine-year-old child with a ballpine hammer can activate the sensors that release the bag while the car is parked and cause the car owner several hundred dollars to have the bag repacked.

tics, the nature of the exercise demands that politicians please other people; in the judiciary, judges are not penalized simply for pleasing themselves.

The traditional political process has achieved a fairly sophisticated compromise in the area of automobile safety. In essence, this compromise involves a decision by the Federal Highway Safety Administration to compel the automobile manufacturers to lobby the state legislatures — a very expensive process — to get mandatory seatbelt usage legislation adopted by 1989. In return, the federal regulators have agreed not to require cars to be equipped with inflatable airbags if a sufficient number of states pass compulsory seatbelt laws by 1989. The day is not far off, however, when a seriously injured plaintiff will win an airbag case in some state court system. When this finally happens, airbags will move from the drawing boards to the dashboards because of the threat of million-dollar tort judgments. The whole political process will have been bypassed. But what about all the cars that were manufactured before the court decision that I predict? If they crash, will the manufacturers be liable? No one knows, but more to the point, no one has budgeted into the car producers' business equations the potential damage awards that such a holding might entail.

The airbag cases are a perfect example of the dangers to business that this book will deal with. Airbag cases are not just private disputes between injured plaintiffs and car producers; they are cases that invite courts to make sweeping general rules about national policy. It is no exaggeration to say that the economic welfare of scores of thousands of workers and the continued vitality of many manufacturing communities are up for grabs in every backwoods state court where one of these airbag cases might be tried. Toppling the apple cart requires nothing more than a plaintiff's verdict in some county courthouse that is later affirmed by a state's highest court. With fifty separate state court systems, the result that I predict is almost inevitable, and once one state allows recovery on the airbag theory, other states will inevitably follow that precedent to protect their own citizens. A Vermont appellate judge is unlikely to be overly concerned about the problems of a Michigan car producer in a case involving a seriously injured Vermont resident.

The spectre of a plaintiff's verdict in an airbag case points out that the political results courts give are often at odds with the political results we get from legislatures. Courts and legislatures are responsive to different constituencies. Legislatures reflect a mélange of special interests — economic, geographic, racial, religious, etc. — and the laws that Congress or a state legislature enacts are a direct function of the respective political strengths of those interests. Courts, on the other hand, staffed as they are by judges who are either life-tenured appointees or elected for very long terms, have no electoral constituencies. The constituency, however, that has the highest impact on judges' decision-making consists largely of those with whom judges most identify socially and politically: lawyers, university professors, and above all, the media. Although state legislators are drawn from all walks of life — teachers, factory workers, railroad engineers, housewives, lawyers, and insurance agents — judges are drawn from only one: lawyers. While the attention of legislators must always be focused on the next election, judges fancy that they are able to focus exclusively on the "public good." Judges, then, aspire to place themselves above politics and enter the world of statesmanship.

Often the perceived "public good" is simply a function of whatever received wisdom and other ideological baggage a judge has brought with him or her to the bench. I point this out to emphasize that although judges make important political decisions in the United States, they are difficult to influence because they are largely removed from the give and take of the political arena and have no personal incentive whatsoever to accommodate conflicting interests. Unlike other politicians, a judge must be shown the relationship between possible outcomes in a precedent-shattering case and the public good as that good is perceived, perhaps eccentrically, by that particular judge. Unfortunately, what confounds so many businesspeople is that judges' objectivity and willingness to listen are inversely related to the amount of received wisdom or ideological baggage they have brought with them to the bench.

Sadly, in some of business' important cases, the only side that presents all the facts favoring its position is the plaintiff. In an automobile crash case where the lawsuit is based on lack of airbags, for example, the plaintiff will be there in a wheelchair, and any judge will easily understand that the plaintiff is a widowed mother of five. The court will also know that the plaintiff has no support but miserly social security payments although she needs full-time nursing attention and child-care services. On the other hand, General Motors is solvent and profitable. Elaborate discussions in an airbag case about the engineering feasibility of airbags, whether the manufacturer could have foreseen the injury to the plaintiff, or whether there is precedent or a lack of precedent supporting a recovery for the plaintiff miss the human dimension: In the individual case at hand General Motors can afford to help the injured plaintiff and pass the cost along to all General Motors customers or stockholders.

To win an airbag case on behalf of General Motors, then, it is necessary to make as compelling a *human* case *against* airbags as the plaintiff is making for individual help. This latter undertaking involves showing the consequences to employment in the automobile industry if the price of cars is increased to provide airbags. How many jobs, for example, will be affected if the high cost of airbags drives 150,000 buyers out of the market in a given year? What is the potential liability of manufacturers for accidents occurring in cars made before the court's airbag ruling if that ruling is retroactive? What will be the effect on employment of diverting money from investment into the payment of damage awards? All of these issues are what political science professors call "legislative facts"; they have little to do with precedent or what businesspeople usually think of as law, but it is these issues that impress policy-making judges. Although this type of information may not be admissible before a jury, it can be made part of the record in the trial court on the grounds that it will be relevant on appeal to the issue of what the law should be.

In the precedent-shattering cases what really counts seldom has anything to do with technical legal rules; appellate judges, in my thirteen years of experience, are remarkably unimpressed with scientific/academic legal principles unless those principles lead where, for policy reasons, the judges want to go.[5] Appellate courts have sweatshops of clerks with sterling academic credentials who can cobble up craftsmanlike legal opinions justifying almost any result. There is, indeed, at least sparse legal precedent for almost any proposition, no matter how absurd.

Appellate courts, in precedent-shattering cases, look at legislative facts, not law. If legislative facts are not presented to them by the parties in some authentic and understandable form, the judges can base their decisions on the real or imagined legislative facts that they can conjure up from their own life experience. Once appellate judges have decided what they *want* to do, their law clerks can cut and paste the appropriate legal principles necessary to justify the result.

Of course, judges don't always do whatever they want in every lawsuit that comes before them. Fortunately, a high percentage of policy-making judges regard stability and predictability in the law as desirable qualities, which means that many judges *want* to follow precedent. But as a general rule, the greater the public consequences of a particular judicial decision, the higher the likelihood that judges will make their decisions on social policy grounds rather than the narrow grounds of legal precedent.

For example, during the last fifteen years challenges have been made all over the United States to the way that states administer local property taxes. Because the property tax is the basic vehicle for

---

[5]Were this not the case, how could the supreme court of Alaska have legalized the use of marijuana by Alaska residents in the face of an explicit Alaska statute making marijuana use illegal?

funding local government — particularly schools — constituencies
wanting expanded social services have looked for ways to circumvent conservative legislatures to get more revenue into the coffers
of local governments and school boards. Lawyers for the plaintiffs
in these cases figured out that if they could convince the judges of
the highest state courts that more money was needed for schools
and deserved, the judges would not be reluctant to allow themselves to be used to make an end run around parsimonious legislatures. Many of these cases were successful, even though few were
founded on what most experienced lawyers would consider solid
legal ground.

In 1982 West Virginia had a local revenue case that challenged
the administration of our property tax. A school board that wanted
more money argued that the way its county's locally elected assessor
calculated property taxes was illegal. The board's argument was
based on language in the West Virginia constitution that said "property shall be assessed at its true and actual value." In 1953, however,
the state legislature had passed a statute allowing assessors to cal-
culate property taxes on any appraisal they wished between 50 percent and 100 percent of true market value.[6] The result of this statute,
combined with the reluctance of locally elected county assessors to
raise their constituents' taxes, was that most counties put property
on their books at about 50 percent of market value — a practice on
which capital- and land-intensive industries had relied since 1953.
Furthermore, in *two previous* state supreme court opinions the court
had sanctioned less-than-market-value assessments, which led to

---

[6]One of the major practical problems in assessing property taxes is that
property values fluctuate widely from year to year. A rise in interest rates,
for example, will reduce the market value of private houses. Commercial
property will be affected not only by interest rates but also by the business
cycle. Assessing property on something less than actual market value
avoids constant litigation about what property is worth from year to year,
which is one legitimate reason that this system is common almost everywhere. If more revenue is needed, from a practical point of view, it is
better to raise the rates but continue to assess less than market value.
Unfortunately, this avenue is closed because states usually limit the rate
of property tax in their constitutions — difficult instruments to change.

further reliance on the time-honored practice. If law followed academic or scientific principles, the validation of less-than-market-value assessment by earlier courts would have disposed of the 1982 case, and this was what the business lawyers defending less-than-market-value assessment argued. But they were rudely awakened!

No issue before today's courts is ever definitely decided by the opinions of yesterday's courts. Between 1977 and 1985 a "liberal" majority commanded the West Virginia Supreme Court of Appeals, and that majority was passionately committed to better schools. The plaintiff school board understood that the level of property taxes is a political issue and that a court of comparatively young men elected in the late 1970s was unlikely to be controlled by the decisions of judges who were old when the sitting judges were in grade school. The plaintiffs expected to convince a majority of the court that a blow for civilization could be struck by increasing the money for schools — a blow that could never be struck in the legislature.

The West Virginia Supreme Court of Appeals bought the plaintiffs' argument and held that the constitutional language "true and actual value" meant current fair market value. In most counties that decision required *doubling* property taxes. Fortunately for business taxpayers, the legislature immediately convened in special session to draft a constitutional amendment that watered down the decision. Taxes, however, still went up because legislators who wanted more money for schools demanded concessions in return for passing the constitutional amendment. The constitutional amendment allowed taxes to be raised but spread the increase over ten years.

The West Virginia property tax case touched on matters of supreme importance to numerous constituencies in West Virginia: It directly affected business costs, homeowner taxes, the attractiveness of West Virginia as a site for new industrial plants, the quality of the state's schools, and the operating budget of every county commission in the state. Yet the process by which a decision controlling such weighty matters was made in the courts was entirely different from the process that would have controlled a subject of similar importance in the legislature.

A proposal to double property taxes in the West Virginia legislature would have stimulated protests to local legislators by every business. Some of those protests would have amounted to little more than outraged yelling and screaming, but major businesses would have sent persuasive lobbyists to show how higher property taxes lead to a general deterioration in the business climate and reduce aggregate employment. Legislators not only would have had heavy constituent pressure from homeowners, but they also would have been forced to analyze whether higher property taxes would put West Virginia business at a competitive disadvantage vis-à-vis business in other states. When, however, the tax issue was presented to the state supreme court, the litigants — namely the Logan County board of education as plaintiff and the Logan County assessor as defendant — presented simplistic briefs that focused almost exclusively on the language of the state constitution and the prior opinions of the state supreme court. Although the issue to be decided was one of important public policy, the case was argued entirely in the scientific/academic language of private disputes — as if the court were being asked to decide a contract case between Sears and a supplier of television sets.

Whenever a court is to decide an issue that has broad social implications for parties who are not before the court, the court will allow individuals, unions, business groups, or just about anyone else who has an interest in the outcome of the case to file *amicus curiae* (friend-of-the-court) briefs to inform the court of the effect of possible decisions on parties who are not involved in the specific litigation. In the Logan County tax case a few business associations filed friend-of-the-court briefs that were marginally better than the briefs submitted by the parties; however, even the lawyers for big business focused on what can loosely be called "legal" questions — what the words "true and actual value" mean, the legal effect of the time-honored system of taxation that may be evidence of the intention of the constitution's draftsmen, and whether prior court rulings on the issue were decisive. No one who provided an *amicus* brief addressed the possibility of bankruptcy for marginally profitable businesses because of unexpected and unbudgeted taxes, or the different effects that this particular type of tax — namely, a regressive property tax — would have on land and capital-intensive employers who were able to relocate to other states to avoid these extra taxes.

Furthermore, the Logan County tax case was treated exactly like every armed robbery, child custody, or automobile accident case that our court decided in the spring of 1982. The petitioners had half an hour to present their arguments orally, and the respondents had twenty minutes. The trade associations that filed *amicus* briefs were not allowed to argue orally, nor was any judge or law clerk compelled to read their briefs. If my recollection is correct, the court decided about thirty-five cases the week the tax case was decided — the average number we decide every week that we sit. Thus the tax case could not have consumed more than an hour of discussion in the court's conference. The thing that was utterly remarkable about the court process, however, was that two inadequately funded and thus inadequately represented parties, the Logan County board of education and the Logan County assessor's office, represented the interests of everyone whom the decision would likely affect.[7]

The Logan County tax case or an airbag case comes into court with a big sign on it indicating that the case is there to change the law. But many other cases end up changing the law simply as the result of a private lawsuit that no one expected to be of any great consequence to anyone except the parties to the suit. Big cases can sneak up on everyone. This may happen either because a host of other, routine-looking issues obscure the legal issue liable to do the most damage or because people simply aren't paying attention. Since tax cases are of interest to almost every business, let me explore this problem with another tax case — specifically the U.S. Su-

---

[7]Logan County is a rural coal mining county in southern West Virginia. Its largest town, Logan, has 3,029 people, and the population of the entire county is 50,679. Other than coal mining there is little industry in Logan County; the highly industrialized areas and therefore the areas most affected by the tax decision are in distant counties along the Kanawha, Ohio, and Monongahela rivers.

preme Court's famous *Thor Power Tool* case, which many business-people will remember completely changed how worthless inventory is written off for tax purposes.

Before *Thor* business wrote off worthless inventory in the year it became worthless, and if it were sold later the write-off was recaptured in the tax year of the sale. Since *Thor*, however, worthless inventory can be written off only when it is either sold or scrapped.[8] Among other consequences, this little decision had the effect on book publishers of making it uneconomical to keep older books in print. But to my knowledge the publishing industry was generally unaware that the issue was being litigated; the news arrived when the tax lawyers reported the *fait accompli*.

Thor has many of the attributes of an ordinary, non–precedent-shattering lawsuit. In *Thor* the IRS was pursuing a company that had used shoddy accounting methods to avoid taxes under the old inventory rules. But getting back taxes from Thor Power Tool did not necessarily demand revision of the old inventory rules — a revision that affects all businesses. I suspect that if Thor Power Tool had been less stubborn, the case would have been settled at an early stage through payment of some percentage of the disputed claim. Usually the perennially understaffed IRS just wants money, so I doubt that they set out originally to use Thor's tax liability as a vehicle for remaking the law on inventory.

We have already made a distinction between routine lawsuits and lawsuits that present novel issues and invite courts to change the law. *Thor Power Tool*, however, points out an additional distinction between lawsuits that can be settled versus lawsuits that cannot be settled. Cases like *Thor* that go on to make disastrous law for

---

[8]This "write-down" is of crucial importance to companies that manufacture products requiring replacement parts. To economize on the production of such parts, a manufacturer will produce its anticipated requirement all in one "run" to avoid costly retooling. This practice ensures the availability of replacement parts, but it also ensures that some parts will be overproduced. The manufacturer will eventually scrap these excess parts, but there is a twilight in which the part is still in demand but not in great demand. It is during this interim that Thor tried to write down the value of the parts it was eventually going to scrap.

business often can be settled at an early stage for comparatively little money. New theories of law are usually not advanced on the basis of principle but simply as a device to get money for one side or the other. Strange as it may seem at first, the U.S. legal system is not set up to litigate lawsuits: It is set up to settle lawsuits. Roughly 94 percent of all suits filed in court are settled before trial, and this figure does not include all of the potential lawsuits that are settled after lawyers have been contacted but before formal papers have been filed in courts. Settlements, of course, are predicated on the litigant's expectations about what will occur in court if the case actually goes to trial. Plaintiffs settle because they want money today and cannot support the expense or bear the risk of going to court, while defendants settle because after a certain point they want to save lawyer and court costs and because they are terrified of judges and juries.[9]

---

[9]Procedurally, a plaintiff is required to prove its case by a preponderance of the evidence — a long and expensive process that many a deserving plaintiff cannot underwrite. Once, however, a plaintiff manages to survive the burdensome proof-generation process with all its expensive depositions and costly fast-gun-for-hire expert witnesses, a jury may have unbridled discretion to award outrageously high damages. The more complicated and expensive the procedure, the quicker and cheaper defendants can settle lawsuits, and when the game centers in procedural technicality, money — as profligately and indifferently spent as possible — works miracles. Huge law firms, billing for every hour spent, maintain stables of salaried young lawyers cheerfully churning out obstructive paperwork that buys delay after delay. The sophisticated players in this game understand that the goal is to influence how cases are *settled*, not to influence how 6 percent of all cases filed — the ones that are tried — finally come out.

But many of the cases that most directly affect business cannot be settled. How, for example, can General Motors settle an airbag case without doing itself as much damage as losing the case in court? How can R. J. Reynolds Tobacco settle a lung cancer case without inviting thousands more? How can a major employer pay off a fired employee who has threatened to sue under one of the emerging theories of unlawful discharge without reducing management's prerogatives to the same extent that they would be reduced had the case been lost in court? Business must win these types of cases, but they must win them in the policy-making appellate courts where cogent analysis, statistical information, and artful presentation — not firepower — counts. In the great lawmaking cases — no matter how much money is spent or how long the cases are delayed — what goes on in the trial courts is mere overture.

One of the most intractable problems the court system presents to business is the system's decentralized nature. Decentralization means that business must defend against attack along a broad perimeter, and if we look for a moment at automobile crash cases and employee firing cases we will see that different types of cases present different strategic problems. In the airbag cases there are only a few possible defendants — General Motors, Ford, Chrysler, American Motors, and the foreign producers. Whenever an airbag case is filed in any U.S. court, a red flag goes up throughout the industry. In airbag and similar precedent-shattering cases like the lung cancer cases against tobacco companies, an entire industry cooperates; all companies share information, exchange expert witnesses, and even send specialized lawyers into the fray to help defend the competition. Employee firing cases, on the other hand, are an entirely different proposition.

Even the smallest state has thousands of employers, and all of those employers have at-will employees. In addition, there are fifty-two separate U.S. jurisdictions (including the District of Columbia and Puerto Rico) in which precedent-shattering decisions on employment tenure can be rendered. Many of the employers against whom employment cases are filed do not have money for talented lawyers and protracted litigation. Yet a suit brought by a warehouse employee against a small, nonunionized wholesale grocer in northern Michigan may create precedent that will shatter traditional employee relations throughout General Motors. General Motors, however, may not know about the case until the decision is rendered and the damage complete. General Motors, then, with all its legal resources, would be at the mercy of strategy and resource allocation decisions made by some small enterprise managed by high school graduates!

At this point, it is likely that the reader is saying to himself or herself that the solution to these problems is for the courts to stay out of the lawmaking business. As we see later in the book, the courts make law favorable to business all the time, but business often loses sight of the fact that low-visibility, pro-business court decisions concerning the enforcement of rights that Congress or the state legislatures have created are as important as the rights themselves.

For example, in 1936, when Congress passed the National Labor-Management Relations Act (Wagner Act) authorizing and protecting union organizing, Congress created the National Labor Relations Board to enforce the act and supervise labor management relations in the United States. The Wagner Act prohibited certain "unfair labor practices," such as firing an employee for union activity, but the act was not explicit about how the unfair labor practices part of the act should be enforced, except that it *could* be enforced by the National Labor Relations Board. Many union lawyers thought that the Wagner Act allowed illegally fired employees to go to court and sue for damages if they preferred that path to going to the board. One could read the act that way. But the U.S. Supreme Court reviewed this issue in numerous cases for ten years after the Wagner Act was passed and consistently held that the National Labor Relations Board had *exclusive* jurisdiction over unfair labor practices and that employees could not go either to federal or state court.

To this day left-wing lawyers argue that pro-business, conservative courts sold out labor's whole victory in the Wagner Act by consigning enforcement of unfair labor practices to an overworked, understaffed administrative tribunal with cumbersome procedures and limited enforcement powers. When the board hears a case of wrongful discharge because of union activities, it is limited to reinstating the employee with back pay. In a regular lawsuit originating in a trial court, however, the employee would be entitled to his actual damages — such as back pay, the cost of relocation to find a new job, any loss he took on the sale of his house, damages for aggravation and humiliation, plus punitive damages for the infliction of an intentional wrong! If the U.S. Supreme Court had decided that the National Labor Relations Board was not the exclusive enforcement agency, labor's power relative to management would have been enhanced enormously. Many employers have kept unions out of their companies for fifty years simply by firing union organizers, keeping the case in litigation for five or more years until the employee (who was usually blackballed) was forced to move away, and then cheerfully paying the limited back-pay award! If the Supreme Court had ruled that employees could go directly to court, this would probably not have happened, but employers would have been plagued with suits by disgruntled employees whose grievances were totally unrelated to union activity but who claimed unfair labor practices.

The next chapter explains how the courts are organized, the difference between state and federal courts, and a number of other mechanical aspects of the court process. The four chapters after that will try to give as balanced a picture as possible of the forces that are driving the courts into the governing business. They lay an indispensable foundation for exploring how business can improve its track record among judicial lawmakers.

Chapter 2

The Short Course
on Courts

Most high school *teachers and college instructors are* bored to tears by courts. In my high school civics class we spent two fascinating months studying the United Nations and one tedious week studying the entire U.S. judicial system. Therefore, unless the reader attended law school or majored in government in college, his or her knowledge of courts probably comes from personal and idiosyncratic experiences. The mosaic that results from such on and off brushes with the courts, however, is more likely to mislead than to illuminate, and so this chapter on the mechanics of the court system is necessary homework before more interesting matters can be explored.

Unlike most civilized nations, the United States does not have one court system but rather fifty-three separate and distinct court systems. There is (1) the nationwide federal court system, (2) the state court systems of the fifty separate states, and (3) court systems that do the work of state courts in the District of Columbia and Puerto Rico. Administratively these fifty-three separate court systems are entirely independent, and each of the fifty state court jurisdictions is free to enact eccentric decisional law or render idiosyncratic judicial decisions as long as those laws or decisions do not offend either the U.S. Constitution or a specific federal statute.

Perhaps a real case will make the problem of fifty-three separate court systems spring to life. Two residents of West Virginia set off in a car for a destination in the Midwest where the driver was going to look for a job. Her friend was simply along for the ride. While traveling through Indiana, the two West Virginia travelers had a one-car accident in which the driver's friend was severely injured. In West Virginia, if the driver of a car is negligent and causes injury to a passenger, the passenger can sue the driver. In Indiana, however, as the result of an "automobile guest statute," a guest passenger in a car cannot sue the driver for injuries sustained as the result of the driver's ordinary negligence.

Notwithstanding the Indiana law, however, the injured West Virginia passenger sued the driver (who was insured) in West Virginia, and the lawsuit presented the question whether the law of the forum state, West Virginia, or the law of Indiana where the injury occurred should apply. The substantive rule of law that governed the parties at the time that the accident occurred was the Indiana guest passenger statute. Yet the forum state, West Virginia, was asked to apply the law of *West Virginia* on the grounds that both travelers were West Virginia residents; that the trip began and was to end in West Virginia; and that the state of Indiana had absolutely no interest in the subject matter of the litigation other than having been the place where the accident occurred. At the time of this writing, the case is still in the West Virginia supreme court awaiting decision.

Traditionally, it is in the discretion of the courts of the forum state to determine which of two conflicting bodies of law applies to lawsuits brought in the forum state. In fact, determining which of two conflicting bodies of law applies is a separate category of court-made, decisional law known as "conflict of laws doctrine." In the present example, the West Virginia court can decide to apply the law of the state where the accident occurred (on the ancient theory that the law of the place of the accident governs), or it can apply West Virginia law (on the modern theory that West Virginia has the most "contacts" with the litigants and has the strongest interest in seeing that its law is applied to protect its citizens). But as the reader can quickly see, it conceivably makes a great deal of difference whether this case is tried in West Virginia or in Indiana because not only do we lack a national system of courts, but also the separate court systems do not even aspire to behave as if they were a national system. Courts frequently disregard the law of other states if they disagree with that law and search for lame justifications to apply their own policies through their own law.

There is more unity within the federal court system. Federal courts, at least, all have the same boss. Federal judges are appointed by the president for life, are paid by the federal government, are housed in federal office buildings, and have staffs composed entirely of federal employees. State judges, on the other hand, do not receive their marching orders from Washington D.C. State courts are organized according to the dictates of the fifty separate state constitutions, and state judges are paid and supported logistically entirely by the states. The state court equivalents in the District of Columbia and Puerto Rico are created by specific federal statutes; however, the judges of these courts are not "federal judges" but rather locally appointed judges of courts enforcing only local law.

One can find a state court in every county seat in the United States. On the other hand, the 485 federal district court judges are sparsely scattered over eighty-nine district courts in the fifty states. Every state has federal district court judges in proportion to both the population and the volume of litigation. Nevada, for example, has two federal district court judges, while New York has forty. A federal district court judge will either be in residence or regularly visit almost every U.S. city with 100,000 or more people, and federal district courts often sit in very small towns.[1]

In theory the federal judiciary and the state judiciaries perform different functions. General jurisdiction state trial court judges are supposed to handle most U.S. litigation and therefore outnumber federal district judges by at least ten to one in every state. Federal courts are courts of *limited* jurisdiction, and they decide only cases

---

[1]E.g., Fergus Falls, Minnesota, population 12,514, Charlottesville, Virginia, population 45,010, and Coeur D'Alene, Idaho, population 20,054.

arising under *federal* law or cases arising between citizens of different states. This latter type of jurisdiction, known as "diversity jurisdiction," is designed to give out-of-state litigants a slightly fairer shake than they might get in their adversary's home state court. In many states, local voters elect state court judges, and that leads to the daunting suspicion that these judges might be susceptible to local political pressures. But because federal judges enjoy life tenure, federal judges are allegedly immune from venal parochial influences and are less likely than state judges to serve "home cooking" to out-of-state litigants.

In practice almost every defendant and many plaintiffs would like to get into federal court. Federal judges are better paid than state judges,[2] their courtrooms and supporting staffs are usually superior to those of the state courts, and federal judges are usually better educated and more thoughtful than their state counterparts.[3] There are many exceptions to these generalizations, but the pervasive public perception is that the United States' top-drawer, class courts are the federal district courts. Yet this popularity is not an unmixed blessing for federal judges. Attorneys stay up nights figuring out ways to wangle their cases onto the federal courts' dockets, while federal judges stay up nights figuring out ways to keep these cases out. Judges, it must be remembered, do not enjoy extra work any more than posthole diggers!

---

[2]U.S. Supreme Court justices earned $100,600 a year in 1985. Judges of the federal circuit courts of appeals earned $80,400, and federal district court judges earned $76,000. State supreme court salaries ranged from $93,084 in Alaska and $92,500 in New York to $53,308 in Oregon. State trial court judges got a high of $86,504 in Alaska to a low of $46,000 in Vermont. As a general rule, however, state judges earn only about 75 percent of the salary of their federal counterparts.

[3]Part of the reason for the difference in qualifications has to do with the sample from which federal judges may be drawn. Not only are federal judges paid close to a living wage for skilled lawyers, but federal judges enjoy surpassing prestige. While being a state court judge often involves running regularly for office or at least surviving retention elections, once a person is appointed a federal judge he or she can sit on the bench for life (and many federal judges are in their eighties). Although a high percentage of successful lawyers would turn down appointments to state courts, few turn down federal judgeships.

In diversity cases, for example, federal courts require that there be total diversity among the parties to a lawsuit before a federal judge will touch the case. Therefore, if a New York corporation brings one lawsuit against three joint defendants — a New Jersey corporation, a Delaware corporation, and one New York individual — the New York individual on the defendants' side destroys diversity and removes federal court jurisdiction, even though the individual may be only a nominal defendant. Plaintiffs' lawyers who want to be in a state court — either because it is quicker and cheaper or because they smell the aroma of tasty home cooking — are very artful in developing techniques to destroy federal diversity jurisdiction, and because federal courts are overworked, federal judges aid and abet that enterprise.

In a similar vein, although federal courts decide cases arising under federal law, they will accept a case only if the *original plaintiff's complaint* asserts a *claim* under federal law. By contrast, if a defendant asserts a *defense* arising under federal law, there is no federal jurisdiction. For example, if a plaintiff sues a newspaper for libel under state libel law, the plaintiff has asserted a state cause of action and must bring suit in state court (unless the plaintiff and the newspaper happen to be residents of different states). If the newspaper defends on the grounds that what was written was privileged under the first amendment to the United States Constitution, the case must still stay in the state court because federal law defenses do not confer federal court jurisdiction.

There is a way for the federal courts to review state ajudications of federal rights through appeal from the highest court of a state to the Supreme Court of the United States. This theoretical federal control of state court decisions about federal matters gives rise to the blustering threat "I'll fight you all the way to the Supreme Court!" Usually the threat is empty. The only way to go from the highest court of a state into the federal system (except in criminal cases) is to show the U.S. Supreme Court that the state court system misapplied a federal law principle and that the case involves an important matter of federal policy. Thus vague assertions that the fourteenth amendment's due process clause was violated are unlikely to inspire Supreme Court review because the Supreme Court is concerned only with bad principles of law and not bad judgment calls.

The slender thread that holds the fifty-three separate court systems together in this country is the Supreme Court of the United States, and therefore the Supreme Court's highest priority is to impose order and uniformity on a diverse and sometimes chaotic federal/state system. The U.S. Supreme Court decides only about two hundred cases a year and has an arsenal of procedural devices for avoiding cases it does not want to hear. The Supreme Court is not in the business of rendering customized, individual justice to all litigants; rather, it reserves itself for important cases of national policy.

In the federal court system, and the court systems of the more populous states, the court system is three tiered. (There is also a fourth tier of minor courts that will be discussed below.) At the base of the judicial pyramid are the general jurisdiction trial courts. In these courts a single trial judge presides over all the proceedings that we generally associate with "going to court." There may or may not be a jury depending on (1) whether a jury is asked for and (2) whether the case presents a legal issue or an equitable one.[4]

From the trial court litigants ascend to the first appellate level, which in the federal system is called the circuit court of appeals and in the state systems is usually called the intermediate court of appeals. The purpose of the federal circuit courts and state intermediate appellate courts is to do customized, individual justice for all litigants who appeal; everyone who is dissatisfied with the decision in a trial court has an absolute right to appeal the adverse decision to the intermediate appellate courts. However, a litigant must stay in the system that he or she starts out in. Thus state trial court rulings cannot be appealed to federal circuit courts, and federal district

---

[4]The difference between law and equity is something that few law students understand entirely after graduating from law school; I will attempt to explain the subtle difference later in this chapter.

court rulings cannot be appealed to state intermediate appellate courts.

The issues that appellate courts consider are very narrow because an appeal is not an opportunity to do the whole case over again before a different judge or judges. In any appeal the litigants are limited to discussing what they presented in the trial court. New witnesses, new evidence, and new theories cannot be conjured up and presented to the appellate court for the first time to strengthen a case on appeal. The appellate courts are interested only in whether some error was committed by the trial court. These errors typically involve improper instructions to the jury, the admission of evidence that should have been excluded, or an incorrect ruling on a matter of law.[5] Many appellate arguments resemble the arid debates of the medieval scholastic philosophers. In an appellate court there is never a jury, a live witness, or even an impassioned speech. About the only ingredients that enter into an appellate court proceeding are the lawyers, judges, and papers — thousands and thousands of pages of papers. In fact, appellate courts are so dull that even judges have been known to sleep on the bench.

The role that appellate courts play is tied to a conceptual scheme that divides lawsuits into two parts — facts and law. The facts are what actually happened to the litigants that gave rise to the lawsuit. Was Smith going 10 miles an hour when he hit Jones's car as Smith claims, or was Smith barreling through a red light with the pedal to the floor as Jones claims? Was Johnson the man in the Seven Eleven store at midnight with the ski mask over his face and the shotgun in his hand? Did the underwriter know at the time the stock was offered that the prospectus prepared by the issuer made false material statements of fact? These are typical factual questions that juries decide, and appellate courts are reluctant to overturn a jury's decision about which version of disputed facts transpired in a

---

[5]Criminal cases present a host of additional considerations that revolve around the defendant's constitutional rights to fair treatment by police and prosecutors, and it is from appellate court decisions in this area that the popular controversy about the "exclusionary rule" has sprung.

case. The general rule is that an appellate court will not disturb a jury verdict unless the verdict is contrary to the substantial weight of the evidence. In jury trials, the jury has almost the exclusive power to determine the facts.

Questions of law, on the other hand, are the responsibility of the trial court judge, whose decision about the law is routinely second-guessed by appellate courts. For example, in a libel suit by a politician against a newspaper, it makes no difference how untrue or how damaging the newspaper's story was if the newspaper believed the story to be true. The first amendment protects newspapers from libel actions by politicians unless a politician can show the paper published false material with full knowledge it was false and with a deliberate intent to injure the politician involved through the publication of false material, or that the paper published a false statement in "reckless disregard" of the truth. Consequently, when a libel action is submitted to the jury, the trial court must properly instruct the jury that before the plaintiff can recover against the newspaper the jury must find that (1) false material was published; (2) the newspaper knew or should have known the material was false; and (3) the newspaper had a deliberate intent to injure the plaintiff through the publication of false material. If the trial court fails to give a jury such an instruction, an appellate court will reverse a judgment for the plaintiff.

In any lawsuit there are elements that are obviously questions of fact and other elements that are equally obviously questions of law, but most of the time there is also a big grey area where it is difficult to pigeonhole an issue as either factual or legal. If we return for a moment to our libel example, what occurs if it is impossible for the plaintiff to prove that a newspaper *knew* information it published was false but the plaintiff can prove the newspaper behaved so recklessly that it is obvious the paper was entirely indifferent to whether the information was true or false? Is a showing of simple negligence sufficient to show "intentional" injury? If you ask members of the average jury they will say yes, but if you ask the justices of the Supreme Court of the United States they will probably say no on a five-to-four vote. Because the Supreme Court runs the system, the question obviously becomes one of law and not of fact, but there is no compelling logic to that conclusion. If you like newspapers, you say that as a matter of law a plaintiff must prove knowing and intentional injury or some egregious recklessness; if you like politicians, you say that the jury can look at the facts and draw its own conclusions about whether the injury was intentional. The bottom line, however, is that any time an appellate court wants to take control of a subject for political reasons, it will characterize whatever issue it wants to control as a question of law.

In general, plaintiffs' lawyers try to conceptualize all the issues in a lawsuit as questions of fact because that gets them to the jury, and juries notoriously have a low threshold of outrage and operate on the emotive principle that the deep pocket pays. Defendants' lawyers, on the other hand, try to conceptualize the issues in a lawsuit as questions of law because that puts the case in the cold hands of the law-bound judge. The more elements of a case that are classified as questions of law, the greater the likelihood the defendant will be able to undermine the jury's verdict on appeal, and the more elements that are classified as questions of fact, the more impregnable a jury's verdict becomes. Furthermore, as long as there are legal issues in dispute, the defendant can keep the case in the courts and keep her money in the bank where it is earning her and not the plaintiff interest. When an appellate court reverses a trial court judgment because of some technical error of law and sends the case back for a new trial, the defendant gets either another bite at the apple in court or a fresh opportunity to offer a low settlement.

In sparsely populated states — places like Vermont, New Hampshire, West Virginia, and Wyoming — there are only two layers of major state courts, and in those states the functions of both the intermediate court of appeals and the highest court of the state are combined in one state supreme court. New York, California, Illinois, Ohio, Maryland, Michigan, and all states that look vaguely like them have both intermediate courts of appeals and a state supreme court.[6] Almost everywhere the highest state court is not required to hear every appeal brought to it. The bigger the state and the higher the volume of litigation, the lower the likelihood that the state's highest court will decide any particular lawsuit.

State supreme courts and even the U.S. Supreme Court occasionally reach down into mundane lawsuits or criminal prosecutions to correct glaring injustices, but in general high-level appellate courts reserve themselves for the "big cases" that involve broad issues. A supreme court's function is political (in the best sense of the word) as well as legal because it must establish policy in those areas in which courts make policy and assure uniformity throughout its particular jurisdiction.

For example, in the federal system there are twelve separate federal circuit courts of appeals responsible for twelve separate geographical areas. The smallest circuit consists of only the District of Columbia, while the largest, the ninth circuit, consists of the states of California, Washington, Oregon, Alaska, Hawaii, Idaho, Nevada, Montana, Arizona, the territory of Guam, and the district court for the Northern Mariana Islands. Each of the twelve separate federal circuits is entirely independent of the others in terms of administration and personnel, and, consequently, different federal circuits will decide important policy matters differently. When a conflict between two or more circuits arises, the U.S. Supreme Court will accept a case that presents the issue that has caused the conflict, decide the issue, and resolve the conflict.

The state intermediate appellate courts that are responsible for separate geographical areas in big states like California and New York — both of which would rank among the world's top 10 industrial powers if they were independent countries — are prone to the same type of conflicts that occur in the federal circuits. Unsurprisingly, the highest courts in big states serve the same conflict-resolving, policy-making functions that the U.S. Supreme Court serves at

---

[6]For historical reasons, in New York the lowest trial court is called the "supreme court," while the highest state court is called the "court of appeals."

the national level. This job is important because in both the state and federal systems new issues arise on a regular basis that should be dealt with as quickly as possible by the jurisdiction's highest court in order to give an authoritative pronouncement to guide future litigation in the lower courts and, more important, out-of-court settlements. Nonetheless, these high courts are so busy fashioning policy that they have little time to deal with the more quotidian problems of most litigants. Although most state litigation ends in a state's intermediate appellate court, the big, precedent-shattering cases will always go all the way up. The same rule applies in the federal system. Routine federal cases end in the circuit courts of appeals, but major issues of policy eventually get to the U.S. Supreme Court.

The final pieces in the court system puzzle are the limited-jurisdiction minor courts. These courts operate outside the three-tiered system that I have just described. The amount of money at stake in these courts does not usually justify extensive appeals with attendant legal costs. Minor courts offer comparatively quick resolution of problems but are a little short on exhaustive due process. Technically, the minor courts constitute a regular level in the court hierarchy directly below the state trial courts or federal district courts.

In the federal system there are federal magistrates who set bond in criminal cases, hold hearings in prisoner habeas corpus cases, assess traffic fines for speeders on military reservations, and otherwise dispose of minor matters. In addition, bankruptcy judges are the powerful adjuncts of the federal district court judges. In the past the status of bankruptcy judges has been problematic. They do not enjoy the status of life-tenured, federal judges, and litigants may appeal a bankruptcy judge's decision to the U.S. district court. But bankruptcy judges wield enormous power over any business entity in financial trouble that seeks shelter under the federal bankruptcy act, and as bankruptcy becomes more prevalent, involving prominent businesspeople, Fortune 500 companies, and even entire nations, the reputation and influence of bankruptcy judges are bound to rise. Bankruptcy judges are narrow specialists, and the federal system has a number of other, similarly specialized courts such as the federal tax court and the federal court of military appeals. In general, however, the federal system does not have a great deal of litigation going on at a level beneath or (in specialized courts) parallel to the federal district court level. The opposite situation, however, prevails in the state courts.

In every state there is some system of minor courts that handles minor criminal matters and civil cases up to some jurisdictional limit — say $2,000 to $10,000. It is impossible to draw any uniform portrait of these courts because their structures and relationships to the higher courts differ dramatically from state to state. In Connecticut, for example, general jurisdiction trial court judges do tours of duty in the minor courts for a certain number of months and then return to general jurisdiction trial court duties. In West Virginia, on the other hand, the judges of the minor courts are laymen who are elected on partisan ballots for four-year terms with no higher educational requirement than a high school diploma. In Florida it is required that urban counties with a certain population have lawyers serve as minor court judges, while in the rural counties lay judges are still allowed. Throughout the different states the minor courts are variously called "district courts," "justice of the peace courts," "magistrate courts," "small claims courts," and "peoples' courts."

The ratio of minor court judges to general jurisdiction trial court judges is usually about three to one, and litigants can appeal from a decision in a minor court to the general jurisdiction trial court judge and from there up the ladder to the courts of appeal. In practice, however, the number of appeals from minor courts is comparatively small because although litigants can prosecute or defend actions in these minor courts without the aid of a lawyer, an appeal usually requires the help of a lawyer. One can get some idea of the relative volume of litigation in minor courts in comparison to major courts simply by thinking of personal experience. Most Americans — except for domestic matters — have never been to a general jurisdiction court as a litigant, witness, or defendant in their lives, but many of us have appeared in some minor court on a traffic ticket, eviction proceeding, or small debt. The bulk of the matters that minor courts handle are open-and-shut cases, and although these courts are interesting to court reformers, they are of limited interest to businesspeople except as collection agencies.

To summarize, we can divide all courts into two groups — federal and state. In each group there are three major divisions — general jurisdiction trial courts sitting with one judge, intermediate appellate courts that usually sit in three-judge panels, and finally the nine-member U.S. Supreme Court or the five-, seven-, or nine-member state supreme courts that usually sit as full courts in every case. In addition to this three-layer hierarchy of major courts there is a system of minor courts in every state and a system of specialized courts, such as the federal bankruptcy courts and federal tax courts, in the federal system. Some states have imitated the federal system and established specialized tax courts or courts of claims that are outside the normal hierarchy, but such courts on the state level follow no particular pattern.

In every lawsuit the issues to be decided break down into two categories — questions of fact and questions of law. Questions of fact are the exclusive province of the jury in cases where a jury trial is allowed, and an appellate court is unlikely to reverse the factual findings of a jury. Questions of law, on the other hand, are decided by the trial court in the first instance and then by the appellate judges on appeal, with no particular deference being given to the trial court's decisions about legal issues. Whether a particular matter is a question of fact or a question of law is often debatable, and the more issues in a lawsuit that can be categorized as legal questions rather than factual questions, the higher the likelihood of reversal on appeal.

There is one more division in the legal process worthy of our attention, and it concerns the distinction between "law" and "equity" that I raised earlier. Law and equity constitute two distinct branches of legal science, but the difference between the two is entirely historical. There is no theoretical or even practical justification for the distinction between law and equity, but irrational as any distinction may appear to be, the distinction is still important.

Our legal system was inherited from England and was firmly in place at the time of the American Revolution. In eighteenth-century England there were two *separate systems* of courts: The first consisted of the common law judges of the Court of King's Bench, while the second consisted of the lord chancellor and his helper, the master of the rolls, and was called the Court of Chancery. For about four hundred years before 1776 either the common law judges or the lord chancellor would handle new legal problems in England as they arose. Because litigation produced substantial revenue for judges, which branch got which piece of the fee-generating action depended on which branch got interested in the subject first and which branch had the political muscle to seize jurisdiction. For example, common law judges always decided cases involving the ownership of real property, while the chancellor always decided cases involving trusts.

England still has different courts and judges to decide legal and equitable matters. We, on the other hand, allow the same judges (except in Delaware) to decide both legal and equitable cases, but we retain much of the historical procedure that relates to each type of case. The most important part of the historical procedure that survives in the U.S. system concerns the right to a jury trial. The U.S. Constitution guarantees the right to a jury trial in all cases that would have been tried in law courts at the time of the Revolution, but not in cases that would have been tried in equity courts at that time. Historically, the equity courts in England did not provide jury trials. Therefore, if a matter was originally equitable in nature, there is no right to a jury in the United States. Some states, like Texas and Georgia, have a peculiar love for juries and have expanded the right to jury trials into matters that historically were equitable in nature. But in the federal system, and in most state court systems, today's courts still honor the distinction between law and equity and do not give jury trials in equity cases.

Happily for those who wish to appeal adverse equitable judgments (even though appellate courts often analogize judge findings in equity to jury findings at law), the factual findings of a judge in an equity proceeding are usually not accorded nearly the weight that a jury verdict is accorded. Some cases present both legal and equitable issues in the same lawsuit, and when this occurs litigants are entitled to a jury trial on the legal issues while the judge alone decides the equitable issues. In divorce cases, for example, neither side is entitled to a jury trial (except in Texas and Georgia) because in eighteenth-century England divorce was not a subject over which common law courts had jurisdiction. In criminal cases, on the other hand, one always gets a jury because criminal cases were handled exclusively by the common law judges of king's bench. Other than divorce, the most important cases on the equity side of the court are injunction proceedings where the petitioner is seeking not a money judgment but rather a court order requiring someone else either to do something or not to do something. In a suit against a business to abate a nuisance, such as heavy smoke or a bad odor, a judge will hear and decide the entire case because the relief sought is equitable in nature — namely, an injunction to abate the nuisance. Similarly, when business goes to court to enjoin an illegal strike, a judge alone will hear the case.

As any reader of Dickens's *Bleak House* is well aware, there is a certain irony in the use of the word *equity* to designate a particular branch of jurisprudence. In common usage *equity* means fairness, but there is nothing inherently fairer or less technical in equity proceedings than there is in proceedings on the law side of the courts. The ideal of equity, of course, has always been that a judge may bend technical rules of law in a court of equity to accommodate egregious factual situations that the legislators could never have foreseen when they promulgated particular general rules. Today, however, equity has as many formal rules as law.

Other than the injunction, the most popular creature of equity still stalking the legal byways these days is the shareholders' derivative suit. A stockholder brings a derivative suit on behalf of the corporation, not to redress a wrong done him individually, but to obtain recovery or relief in favor of the corporation for all similar stockholders and to compensate the corporation as a collective entity for some wrong done to it by management. Thus, the nature of a derivative suit is twofold: First, it is the equivalent of a suit by the stockholders to compel the corporation to sue; and second, it is a suit by the corporation, asserted by the stockholder on its behalf against those liable to it.

Usually a group of stockholders — or a single stockholder, for that matter — seeks to enjoin the managers or directors of a corporation from carrying out a certain course of conduct such as setting up a stock option plan for management, selling certain assets of the corporation, or allowing the corporation to be exploited by its dominant stockholder. Stockholders often try to enjoin an important business transaction. Needless to say, their actions may compromise the deal. Consequently, it is important for corporations to have a forum where they can get these matters adjudicated quickly and clearly. This explains the continuing existence and popularity of the Delaware chancery court. One of the reasons that the tiny state of Delaware continues to be the place of incorporation of over half of the Fortune 500 corporations is that its chancery court has historically provided, and continues to provide, speedy and clear resolution of derivative suits and other related corporate litigation. If jury trials were allowed in these matters, litigation would be endless.

One wins lawsuits either by getting a favorable judgment from a court or by negotiating a favorable settlement out of court. All litigation involves three distinct elements, and to prevail as a plaintiff one must be successful with all three; to prevail as a defendant requires being successful with but one. Briefly summarized, the elements that go into any lawsuit are (1) substantive rules of law; (2) the concrete application of those rules; and (3) the procedure through which the rules are applied. By substantive rules of law, I mean the general rules of conduct that determine a person's liability. For example, it is illegal for an issuer of securities to make false statements of material fact in a prospectus, and it is illegal to fire an employee because she is a woman or a member of a minority. Both legislatures and courts create substantive rules. Historically the courts themselves have made the rules in torts, contracts, trusts, and real property law, and occasionally, as was explained in Chapter 1, Congress or a state legislature will modify court-made rules. Rules that determine the amount of damages recoverable, the grounds for recovery (negligence, defective products, absolute liability for dangerous activities), and the acceptable defenses to an action (like contributory or comparative negligence) are all examples of substantive rules of law.

The second element in any lawsuit involves applying these substantive rules of law to specific sets of facts. It is necessary to take a real-life situation, divide it into separate components, and then fit each component into some preexisting legal category such as negligence or fraud. This matching of concrete facts and abstract legal categories often seems artificial to both layperson and lawyer alike, and two equally well-trained and experienced lawyers will frequently be unable to agree about what general rule fits a specific factual situation because law not only provides a host of general rules but also provides an even greater host of exceptions to general rules.

The last element in a lawsuit, and one that mushrooms in prominence once a dispute actually goes to court, is the procedure used to get a decision. Which party, for example, has the burden of proof? In a criminal case the defendant is presumed innocent, and the state must prove him or her guilty beyond a reasonable doubt. Society prefers to let the guilty go free than take the chance of convicting the innocent. This is a perfectly reasonable policy choice, but it is achieved through *procedure* rather than through any *substantive* rule of law. Similarly, in a civil suit the plaintiff must prove the liability of the defendant, and that makes recovery much more difficult than if the law required the defendant to prove his or her freedom from liability.

When courts or legislatures make new law that turns out to be adverse to business, they often do so by tinkering at the *procedural* rather than the *substantive* side of the the legal system. For example, the major changes in the product liability law in the last twenty years have largely been the result of a restructuring of the burden of proof. To recover for a defective product it is now no longer necessary to prove negligence on the part of the manufacturer; rather, all that a plaintiff must show is that a product is defective, and the law will *presume* negligence. The manufacturer can avoid liability, however, by showing that the defect in the product arose as a result of something that occurred after the product left the manufacturer's control, which places a nearly impossible burden on the manufacturer — while the old rules that the plaintiff had to prove the manufacturer's negligence placed a nearly impossible burden on the plaintiff.

Indeed, the procedural aspects of a case may completely upstage the underlying substantive dispute. In 1985 several Coca-Cola bottlers sued the Coca-Cola Company. The underlying dispute concerned whether the Coca-Cola Company was obligated to sell the bottlers the syrup used in the bottling of the new Diet Coke under the terms of their existing contracts covering the syrup used in the bottling of Coca-Cola. In the pretrial discovery process, the bottlers asked the Coca-Cola Company to divulge the ingredients of secret formula Merchandise 7x. The Coca-Cola Company refused. The company throughout its 100-year history has closely guarded the formula. The only written version of the formula is stored in a bank vault in Atlanta, and the company's board of directors must vote before anyone is allowed to look at it. At any one time, only two people know the formula. The Coca-Cola Company keeps the identities of the two individuals secret and does not allow them both to fly in the same airplane. The company's devotion to the secrecy of the formula is almost religious, and it gave up production in India, a potential market of 550 million people, rather than divulge the formula. The formula is the company's crown jewel.

The bottlers realized that if they could get hold of the formula, they could force a favorable settlement out of the Coca-Cola Company. The bottlers made a motion in their lawsuit against Coke asking the court to compel the Coca-Cola Company to divulge the secret formula and argued that knowledge of the secret formula was necessary for them to prove their case that the old Coke syrup and the Diet Coke syrup were in fact the same product. The Coca-Cola Company was willing to stipulate that the secret ingredients in the old Coke and Diet Coke were the same and fight the case on the basis of the difference in the two products' publicly known ingredients. But the court decided that the stipulation was not enough. Noting that "except for a few privileged matters, nothing is sacred in civil litigation," the court ordered Coca-Cola to divulge the formula. Although the bottlers' motion was a small part of the normal pretrial skirmishes, it probably will have decisive effect on the litigation. Even if the case does not go to trial, the bottlers' settlement demands undoubtedly skyrocketed on the day the court entered its order to divulge.

Artificial rules of evidence pervade the whole process by which a case is proven.[7] Everyone who reads mystery novels or watches television knows about "hearsay" evidence. In general, hearsay is testimony by one witness about what someone else, not present in court, told him or her and given for the truth of the matter asserted. But there are myriad exceptions to the rule against admitting hear-

---

[7]Many of the rules of evidence seem highly artificial and perhaps more of an obstruction to the courts' truth-finding function than an aid. Ambrose Bierce quips in his *Devil's Dictionary:*

Inadmissible: adj. Not competent to be considered. Said of certain kinds of testimony which juries are supposed to be unfit to be entrusted with, and which judges, therefore, rule out, even of proceedings before themselves alone. Hearsay evidence is inadmissible because the person quoted was unsworn and is not before the court for examination; yet most momentous actions, military, political, commercial and of every other kind, are daily undertaken on hearsay evidence. . . . It cannot be proved that the battle of Blenheim ever was fought, that there was such a person as Julius Caesar, such an empire as Assyria.

But as records of courts of justice are admissible, it can easily be proved that powerful and malevolent magicians once existed and were a scourge to mankind. The evidence (including confession) upon which certain women were convicted of witchcraft and executed was without a flaw; it is still unimpeachable. The judges' decisions based on it were sound in logic and in law. Nothing in any existing court was ever more thoroughly proved than the charges of witchcraft and sorcery for which so many suffered death. If there were no witches, human testimony and human reason are alike destitute of value.

say: One can introduce business records entered by unknown clerks
into evidence with no proof other than that they are business records; one can introduce declarations of dying crime victims to anyone; one can introduce confessions to crimes; and finally, one can
introduce utterances by participants or victims in accidents or
crimes overheard by others if the utterance occurred at the time of
the accident or crime. In fact, there are so many exceptions to the
hearsay rule that the exceptions almost swallow the rule. Nonetheless, the rules of evidence can have a decisive effect on the outcome
of a case because it is frequently a close question whether a certain
piece of proffered testimony is admissible.

To win her case a plaintiff must be successful with regard to all
three elements of a lawsuit. She must find some general rule covering her situation that permits her to recover a judgment; she must
characterize the facts of her case to demonstrate that her situation
fits within the general rule allowing recovery; and she must abstract
the real-life facts so that she can present those facts in a way that
fits the evidentiary and other procedural rules of the court. It is useless for a litigant to attempt to prove her case through mountains of
unrefuted hearsay that any reasonable person would accept. If the
requirements of the rules of evidence are not met, the litigant cannot
introduce her evidence and loses her case. There is often, therefore,
a lack of harmony among the three integral parts of the law. A litigant can succeed in two of three parts yet fail in the third — and
therefore fail entirely.

The distinction between substantive and procedural law is vi-
tally important when one studies the courts as *political* entities. Legislatures seldom deal with the procedural rules that apply in the
courts, and even when they do, courts can easily sidestep statutes
covering procedure. For example, in most states, legislatures have
set statutes of limitations for tort actions that are different from
those set for contract actions. One must bring an action for personal
injuries, libel, slander, and certain business conduct made action-
able by statute within two years of the wrongful act, while one need

not bring an action on a contract for five or ten years, depending on whether the contract is oral or written. Recently, however, courts have avoided statutes of limitations in tort cases by characterizing the causes of action as ones arising out of *implied* contracts. In one case a supermarket violated state law by withholding employees' wages to satisfy accounts owed by the employees to the store where the employees worked. (In other words, a violation of the old "company store" act.) Ordinarily the tort statute of limitations governs an action against an employer for violation of such a statute, but because the court in question wanted the plaintiffs to recover, the court held that the state statute had created a *contract* cause of action and allowed the case to proceed.

One can compare substantive law and procedural law to a water pipe equipped with a valve that regulates the water's flow. The pipe is the substantive law, and the valve is the procedural law. It makes very little difference how big the diameter of the pipe is if the person in control of the valve wants to cut off the water. Similarly, if one person in control of the valve is replaced by another person, the flow of water can be changed dramatically without any modification whatsoever in the diameter of the pipe.

Perhaps the most important procedural concern of business is the circumstances under which thousands of unknown plaintiffs, not one of whom has a claim big enough to justify a lawsuit, can be aggregated into a class action. In a class action there are a few nominal plaintiffs who are members of the class, but the suit is usually the entrepreneurial undertaking of a law firm for a contingent fee. In class action cases the most important decision the court must make is whether the alleged claims can be combined into one lawsuit. A decision that the claims cannot be combined will inevitably cause the whole matter to go away because no one plaintiff has enough at stake to justify bringing the suit. Certification of the class, on the other hand, may allow the aggregation of small claims to the tune of scores of millions of dollars — and a 30 percent contingent fee interest in an award of that size definitely justifies some real care and attention by a plaintiffs' law firm.

The class action suit is also a good example of how new substantive policies often arrive cloaked in procedural changes. The class action suit has a 400-year history of providing a practical way to consolidate all claims in one suit when it is impossible to get all the interested parties before the court. But since the rules governing class action were amended in 1966, litigants have increasingly used the class action device to bring certain types of claims that would not otherwise be brought due to litigation economics and other realities. The liberalization of the class action rules opened the courthouse doors to entirely new types of claims and in effect created entirely new types of substantive rights. Whether these new substantive rights are desirable can be debated. But one definitely undesirable side effect of class action liberalization is court-sanctioned solicitation of claims. Anyone who saw Melvin Belli strolling through the streets of Bhopal, India, with his entourage in tow in the days after the disaster at the Union Carbide plant there intuitively understands the solicitation problem.

The final subject that we must touch on is administrative law, which involves the rules and regulations of administrative agencies. Administrative law has elements of both statutory and court-made decisional law in it, and its complexity relates to how these two external elements bear on the rules, regulations, and decisions of each separate administrative agency. Administrative agencies are a comparatively recent creation in U.S. law. Although there were some early administrative agencies (like the Interstate Commerce Commission) before Franklin Roosevelt's administration, the nation's need for some system of government outside the traditional legislatures and courts sprang from the proliferation of governmental responsibilities that arose in the 1930s. The theory of administrative agencies is that neither Congress nor state legislatures can decide every mundane question that arises in government — but legislators can decide through a general statute what they want to achieve and then create an agency with authority to make rules and regulations to carry out that broad statutory directive. The Internal Revenue Service is a good example of the process. The tax provisions of the

United States Code are often ambiguous or incomplete; accordingly, the IRS can issue rules and regulations under the Code explaining how taxpayers should interpret the Code and what a taxpayer must do to avoid challenge by IRS. When, for example, the tax Code says that a businessperson may deduct reasonable travel expenses, the IRS regulations will explain that a person may claim so much a day for food without keeping receipts and that certain types of entertaining while traveling are deductible while others are not.

One may challenge any action by an administrative agency in court on the grounds that it violates the federal or a state constitution, that it is contrary to the agency's statutory mandate, or that the agency did something procedurally improper when it took the challenged action. If one is dissatisfied with an IRS tax regulation, for example, one can take the issue to tax court to see if the regulation is in faithful harmony with the statute. The result of this process of judicial review is that the courts and not the administrators establish the most controversial and important policies of the administrative agencies. When a court establishes a policy for an administrative agency that offends Congress or a state legislature, Congress or the legislature can override that policy by passing a clarifying statute.

There are administrative agencies at the federal, state, and local levels, and one can challenge any action they take in court on some theory or other. The vaguest and yet occasionally the most useful theory (because one can mobilize it when all else fails) is simply that the agency "abused its discretion." The West Virginia supreme court once had a local school board that refused to admit a child to the state-funded kindergarten program because the child's fifth birthday fell three days after September 1, the last date on which the legislature had said in a statute that children reaching five years of age must be admitted. The statute also *authorized* county boards of education to admit younger children to kindergarten but established no guidelines, giving the impression that if boards wanted to cut off children born after September 1 for a year, they could. The court held, however, that the board of education had an obligation to use its discretion to avoid situations like a child's being denied a year's schooling because of a three-day accident of birth and admitted the child to school.

The kindergarten case eloquently stands for the simple proposition that if an administrative agency has decided something important enough to justify hiring a lawyer and going to court, it is possible to have the ultimate question decided by a court. It makes no difference whether the question concerns admitting a child to kindergarten or building a nuclear power plant. Often, of course, the court will decide the issue exactly the way the agency decided it, but nonetheless, the court will *decide* the issue and in so doing change both the nature of the decision-making process and the nature of the decision-maker.

The nature of law is best understood by a businessperson by reference to the internal procedures of large corporations. A senior executive at Eastman Kodak is more valuable to Eastman Kodak than to another corporation simply because he understands the arbitrary procedures (and, just as important, the personalities) of the corporation in which he has experience. Lawyers are simply executives in the public corporation we call "government," and what they know is how to get things done according to that particular corporation's arbitrary rules. I am, for example, far more valuable as a lawyer in West Virginia than I would be as a lawyer in Massachusetts because I know, so to speak, where all the bodies are buried in West Virginia, while Massachusetts is largely a mystery to me.

Many academic fields of study, particularly physics and mathematics, are difficult because as a student progresses in his mastery of the subject questions proceed to higher and higher levels of complexity. Consequently, most of the sciences can be conceptualized as pyramids; ascending the pyramid involves building on a broad-based theoretical and empirical foundation. Law, however, is difficult not because it becomes progressively more complex as we move from inquiry to inquiry but rather because it is extensive. If, indeed, physics looks like a pyramid, law looks like a checkerboard, and the overall quality of any lawyer depends primarily on the number of squares of the board he or she has mastered. However, there is no theoretical or logical relationship between, say, administrative law and domestic relations law. One of my law school classmates is now among the foremost Washington administrative lawyers, yet he is absolutely terrified when asked the simplest domestic relations question at a cocktail party.

These final comments about the nature of law involve both good news and bad news for businesspeople who want to understand law. The bad news is that it is not possible to master a body of theoretical concepts in law and then generalize from those concepts to arrive at solutions to specific legal problems: One must know the specific, eccentric, concrete rules that arbitrarily apply to each specific problem. The good news, however, is that one need not have gone to law school to master any specific square on the legal checkerboard. If a businessperson wants to become an expert in real property law, tort law, or administrative law, all that is required is some extensive reading and some intelligent conversations with a competent practicing lawyer who knows the field well.

Chapter 3

Whence Cometh
Court Power

Businesspeople tend to perceive politics as an exercise in total victory or total defeat. Perhaps this is because they see the political world in terms of right and wrong, where most decisions can be reduced to simple matters of principle. By viewing the world in such Manichean terms, businesspeople commit the "fallacy of the false alternative" by thinking their choices are much more limited than they actually are. Politicians understand that government involves a latticework of competing and conflicting interests where compromise yields the best overall results because total victory at one point may lead to total defeat at another. In politics, therefore, as in business, most things of importance happen at the margin. Businesspeople have no problem understanding this in business; they are elated if profits can be increased by 10 percent in a single year or if the company's overall travel budget can be reduced by 7 percent. But they all too frequently don't understand this principle in politics.

For all the reasons I shall outline in this chapter, it is not possible to reverse the expansion of judge-made law. In fact, it is inevitable that in the next twenty years the courts will become business' most prominent political hazard. But there is a difference between a hazard and a disaster. The following explanation of the political dynamics surrounding the accretion of court power is calculated to explain the etiology of a potentially, but not necessarily, debilitating disease. Understanding how courts are used by adversaries and how judges perceive their own roles cannot help but lead to more rational strategies for reducing court-generated hazards and achieving better results at the margin.

Theoretically, in our system where the courts are the final arbiters of vague clauses in the federal and state constitutions, courts have limitless power. On the political battlefield interpreting constitutions is the heavy artillery, but most of the time courts can control political issues with simple hand-held weapons like the power to interpret loosely drawn statutes and the power to modify the courts' own decisional law in matters like products liability. There are, however, two practical limits to the courts' power to function as an alternative government.

The first practical limit is the logistical capacity of the courts to manage all the issues that people would like them to decide. For example, when courts have taken over city school districts, as Judge W. Arthur Garrity did in Boston, or have tried to run state mental hospital systems, as Judge Frank M. Johnson did in Alabama, they have found that reforming large-scale institutions in the face of passive resistance from legislatures, administrators, and civil service staff is not a function for which courts are particularly well suited. These types of cases require so much time that judges become administrators, and because court resources are scarce, other litigants suffer because courts are effectively shut down for other purposes.

The second limit on court power is the tolerance of the other actors in the political process. Courts are despised by elected officials and bureaucrats because courts offer the possibility of an alternative government — a government entirely independent of elected politics and the professional civil service. There is an impressive array of weapons that outraged elected officials can use against runaway judges, beginning with such minor harassment as failing to appropriate adequate money for judges' supporting staffs, eliminating judges' travel budgets, keeping judicial salaries at the same level through years of inflation, and even taking away judges' parking spaces — and ending with constitutional amendments to reverse court decisions, and even impeachment.

So far most efforts at judge control have been limited to minor harassment. A federal judge has not been impeached since 1936, and the last federal constitutional amendment to reverse a court decision was adopted in 1913 to allow the passage of the federal income tax. At the state level impeachment is as rare as it is at the federal level, but states do adopt amendments to their constitutions with greater regularity. State constitutions speak to low-level, nitpicking issues and not the more timeless issues that the U.S. Constitution frames.

State judges often resign under threat of impeachment, but these cases involve judges who have either been corrupt or have behaved disgracefully. Judges who are habitually drunk are threatened with impeachment, as are the few who become involved in sex or drug scandals. It is rare that a federal judge has such problems, but in the state courts where the pay is low and judges are often elected, integrity problems appear with greater regularity. One should not confuse the threat of impeachment in these circumstances, however, with the threat of impeachment for making unpopular decisions, something that even the most outrageous judges, such as the notorious Miles Lord in Minnesota, can always survive.

Our almost complete failure to use impeachment and constitutional amendments indicates a conspicuous lack of political will. This lack of political will reflects a lack of consensus; effective emasculation of the courts can be achieved only if there is a consensus that the courts have gone too far in *all* directions, and we are very far from such a consensus. Even the most militant critics of the courts do not want courts to stop doing everything that is political. Court critics want courts to stop doing only those things adverse to their own insular interests. In fact, the strength of the courts as powerful political institutions is directly related to the ironic phenomenon that the people who most consistently vilify the courts are also the first to use them for political purposes.

Business, for example, goes to court at the first sign of an adverse decision by an administrative agency. But business' adversaries — environmentalists, for instance — use the courts to twist business into knots whenever business wants a new power plant, coal mine, or downtown development. Business' loud yelps when it gets stung in the courts obscure the fact that business is more often the aggressor than the victim in the court process that controls administrative agencies. Therefore, business is not about to urge any across-the-board structural changes.

Legislators use the courts for their dirty work by passing vague statutes and then blaming the judges for interpretations that adversely affect their constituents. Presidents, governors, and mayors use court decisions as shields against public outrage over such socially explosive issues as abortion and integration. Conservative labor leaders are quietly pleased when the courts control disruptive wildcat strikes. The poor use the courts to expand debtors' rights, and the rich use the courts to protect their property from government confiscation.

As was indicated in the first chapter, courts operate primarily on political and not academic principles. But this is not to use the word *political* in any pejorative sense. Certainly high-level courts are seldom influenced by partisan or factional considerations, and among all the actors in politics, judges have the least to gain personally from their decisions. The political principles on which courts operate are just that — principles. These political principles, however, have very little to do with what most businessmen think of as "law." They have to do with technology, the structure and practical nature of institutions like legislatures and bureaucracies, and economic and political theory.

Parliamentary democracy is slow, cumbersome, expensive and thoroughly corrupt. When people — business in particular — feel that they have urgent problems that the inertia-prone or corrupt machinery of elected government cannot or will not solve, they look for ways to both bypass and short-circuit the standard government process. The courts have the ability to do both, and so they are widely used; the more they are used, the more we get used to them, and the stronger they become. Although it is unfashionable to artic- ulate this analysis, Americans are turning to the courts for political decisions for many of the same reasons that the middle classes in banana republics turn to military juntas.

The public's willing acquiescence in government-by-judiciary is directly related to the judiciary's incomparable reputation for fair- ness and honesty. Few Americans, for example, fear that they will be unjustly convicted of a crime. The media support the courts be- cause the courts are defenders of the first amendment, and rugged individualists support the courts because courts are the guarantors of our right to be eccentric. Although business is outraged over court decisions about products liability, personnel firings, and a host of other matters, business relies on the courts for protection from government regulators. Judges do not jail their political op- ponents, forbid criticism of the government of which they are a part, or make private fortunes for themselves and their families from their positions of power. In effect, then, they do almost everything for us that a military junta could do, without the unpleasant side effects that accompany juntas elsewhere.

Every lawsuit, of course, has a winner and a loser; losers are usually more reserved than winners in their praise for the *wisdom* of the courts. But even losers seldom challenge the *integrity* of our high-level courts. When judicial integrity is challenged, the chal- lenge is almost always made to judges at the lower end of the state court hierarchy. The justice of the peace courts, magistrate courts, and small claims courts have the lowest reputation for impartial jus- tice. Frequently the judges in these courts are laypersons with sparse legal training, and even more frequently these low-level judges are elected for short terms and for that reason are subject to the political pressures that affect other elected officeholders. Of all the courts, the minor courts have the lowest prestige, and often for good reason.[1]

---

[1] I have devoted another book to the detailed exploration of this problem. See R. Neely, *Why Courts Don't Work* (New York: McGraw-Hill, 1983), par- ticularly Chapter 7.

The state general jurisdiction courts are better regarded, but in the twenty-two states where judges are popularly elected there is always the suspicion that politics influences decisions. Appointed state judges or state judges who have secure tenure after election arouse less concern that decisions are influenced by job security considerations. At the apex of the integrity pyramid, however, are the life-tenured federal judges who are isolated from most of the day-to-day turmoil of the jurisdictions in which they sit and who have nothing whatsoever to gain from the decisions that they make. These well-regarded courts, in turn, reflect a luster so bright that the more pedestrian state courts can bask in its glow.

Courts have neither the power of the purse nor the power of the sword. Therefore, judges must capitalize on their prestige to elicit willing compliance with their orders.[2]

Nothing is more important for the success of courts than a perception by litigants that judges are somehow larger than life — priestlike figures applying an arcane but curative science. In fact, the reason that judges wear black robes is that somber robing makes judges look like priests (and during the Middle Ages judges actually were priests). There is even a certain ceremonial similarity between the chief justice's administration of the oath of office to the president and the coronation of the king of England by the archbishop of Canterbury. In this secularized society it is not even unreasonable to infer that some of the moral authority that once belonged to the church has been transferred to the courts. Such Latin as persists in written court opinions and oral court proceedings is left there to give the illusion that decisions emerge from the depths of an inaccessible science rather than from the policy choices of judges.

Most illusions, however, have at least some tenuous relation to

---

[2]The experience of the United States in trying to enforce the drug laws during the last fifteen years shows what happens when willing compliance with duly enacted laws is not forthcoming. It is estimated that 20 million Americans use cocaine at least occasionally and over 50 million are regular or occasional users of marijuana.

reality. The judiciary works hard as an institution to make the lives of real judges comport with the illusion that the institution tries to project. The result is that there is an elaborate ceremony surrounding all court proceedings and the personal lives of judges are severely circumscribed. The most important part of judicial ceremony is that everything must be open: Judges are absolutely prohibited from any communication with a litigant or his lawyer without the presence of the other side.[3]

Elaborate in-court ceremony would be meaningless, however, if judges routinely socialized with litigants and their lawyers. For this reason most high-level judges do not socialize extensively, and when they do venture into society they attempt to avoid the company of lawyers or litigants. It is, of course, almost impossible to avoid all lawyers and litigants, but lawyers have been trained that it is improper to discuss pending cases with a judge when they meet him or her socially. Judges and lawyers who do not observe the ceremonial conventions are subject to the severest possible discipline — disbarment for the lawyer and removal or total disgrace for the judge.

The requirement for openness in court proceedings and the prohibition against informal communication with judges enhance the honesty of courts. But as we shall see in later chapters, it also significantly reduces the flow of information to judges. This is of critical importance to business because business' side of the important, precedent-setting cases requires an in-depth understanding by judges of economics and practical business that cannot be commu-

---

[3]Society's search for a corruption-free political system that does things openly, without personal trades and side-deals, is an ancient one indeed. The requirement of openness in today's judicial "court" is perhaps, an extension of the ideal — seldom achieved — of openness in a king's court. In China, for example, there is this motto

over the emperor's throne in the Imperial Palace in Beijing where, until 1911, the Manchu emperors held court. Loosely translated, the Chinese characters say, "Be open and aboveboard" or "Don't intrigue or conspire."

nicated in the context of any one case. Judge selection, then, is of critical importance to business because judges are frequently forced to rely on what they have learned in life rather than on what they can learn through presentation of a particular important case.

It is difficult to overstate the premium that this society places on honest government. If one pays careful attention to the debate that attends any general election, the most striking feature of that debate is the degree to which it revolves around the *integrity* of the competing candidates. Other societies appear willing to admit that a competent crook may give better overall government than an entirely honest nincompoop, but not the United States. In our local and congressional elections a challenger seldom questions his opponent's substantive decisions during the last term but questions instead his opponent's character. It is almost inevitable, then, that in a society that places its highest political value on personal honesty, the branch of government that appears most honest and open will be the institution of unconscious preference for the decision of important matters.

Comparatively few judges advance from their initial appointments in the judiciary. Being a judge is usually, if not always, a lifetime condition. Although trial judges typically come to the bench at about the age of forty-eight, most policymaking appellate judges arrive in their fifties. As a group big-time judges are generally mature, but they are also tired. They have entered life's final act and are no longer playing to whatever audience originally inspired them, since by the time they become judges most of that audience is either dead or dying. There are no longer members of the opposite sex to admire them, classmates to be impressed by them, or old high school coaches to be taught lessons. The other actors in the political process — particularly at the state level — have an insatiable appetite for publicity, and this leads them to make daily attacks on every target of opportunity they can find. Judges, on the other hand, appear less adolescent than elected officials because they have neither the need nor inclination to pick fights.

The judiciary is the only branch of government that requires the person making a decision to do his or her own work: Judges must personally sit on the bench, hear oral arguments, listen to the testimony of witnesses, make their own findings of fact and law, and ultimately sign their own names to orders rendering decisions. To the extent that age, maturity, and experience are actual criteria in selecting judges, the system of selection by itself adds a legitimacy based on quality that cannot be duplicated elsewhere.[4]

Although judges have clerks and occasionally individuals known as "masters" or "commissioners" to take testimony, analyze documents, and do wood-hewing and water-carrying in complex cases, most of the time (and always in jury trials) judges hear and read everything of importance themselves. Of course, judges have differing ideas of what is "important." But in the executive branch decisions are made by entire independent divisions, and in the legislative branch most of the voluminous technical work is, out of necessity, done by the young professional staff of legislative committees. The judiciary is not even subject to the normal temptations of empire building because everything must ultimately be done by the judge. The personal staff of a U.S. Supreme Court justice consists of only one secretary and four law clerks! Compare that to the personal staff of a senator or even a humble, small-town major.

---

[4]Throughout the administrative bureaucracy, for example, senior officers mindlessly approve what their juniors place in front of them without giving a great deal of detailed attention to the quality of the product. Several years ago the quality-control problem of regulatory bureaucracies was forcefully brought home to me while I was having a late night coffee at a little restaurant in Caen, France. At a neighboring table were two young Americans who were vacationing, one of whom was a big-firm lawyer who had spent two years with the Department of Transportation. Both of these young men were complaining that their vacation was being dominated by their need to learn how to drive the stick-shift car they had rented. In the interest of helping them along, I drew them a picture of a car's clutch mechanism so that they would understand the physics of the sliding plates that come together when the clutch is released. The young alumnus of the Department of Transportation commented that I had taught him more about cars in twenty minutes than he had learned at the Department of Transportation in two years, although one of the things he did at DOT was to draft safety standards, including safety standards for transmissions!

The practical businessperson who has just read the preceding five paragraphs may by now be amused by the paradigmatic judges that I have just described: Unfortunately, I have never met one of my paradigmatic judges either, nor have I seen a court system that faithfully reflects all of the desirable characteristics of courts that I have just listed. The point, however, is not that judges as individuals or court systems as institutions conform perfectly to the ideal but that court systems and judges conform at least in part to the ideal. As Adolph Berle told me twenty years ago: The exercise of real power always *tends* to conform to the ideological substructure that supports that power.

The ideological substructure supporting court power ascribes a high level of integrity, intelligence, and diligence to judges. Judges in turn strive, albeit imperfectly, to realize those characteristics. They may fail; but the difference between courts and other governmental institutions is that the ideological substructure supporting other institutions demands qualities different from integrity, intelligence, and diligence. No United States senator, for example, would return to his state and admit that he had allowed a defense contract in that state to be cancelled because the weapons system was redundant. And if he did, constituents might give him high grades for integrity, but they would still vote him out of office! In the other branches of government personal honesty may be highly valued, but personal integrity that takes money out of constituents' pockets is not.

Courts have probably been chosen for an expanded lawmaking role not only because of their prestige but also because they are more adaptable than other political institutions in solving problems at this particular stage of our development.[5] Among those problems is a technology, increasingly widespread and complex, that has

---

[5]For much of what follows I am indebted to the careful analysis of the prestigious Council on the Role of Courts published in J. Lieberman, ed., *The Role of Courts in American Society*, (Minneapolis: West Publishing Co., 1984).

made society ever more interdependent. Additionally, in the last twenty years our consensus on the proper distribution of wealth and power in the community has changed dramatically. The most obvious beneficiaries of this transformed consensus are blacks, women, and the poor, but there are more subtle changes as well that rearrange older, time-honored power relationships.

The divorced household, for example, is now as acceptable as the married household. This moves an unprecedented number of family matters into the hands of the courts.[6] Sources of moral authority, such as churches, parents, employers, and schools, that exercised great influence twenty years ago when we were a more traditional society are declining in strength as the United States becomes less cohesive. This, in turn, leads people to the courts to solve problems that formerly were solved elsewhere. The need for regulation has placed more aspects of everyone's life at the mercy of anonymous and unconcerned bureaucrats who, so far, can be brought to heel only by the courts.

The efficiencies of large-scale enterprise have augmented the power of professional management at the expense of individual ownership because large-scale enterprise requires a modern corporation, and modern corporations are seldom managed by their owners. Corporations, however, are divorced from traditional sources of community control, so people go to court to get the attention of policymaking management half a continent away. In this latter regard it must be remembered that about 94 percent of all cases filed in court never go to trial. Today in the United States filing a lawsuit has become a way of signaling to some distant, organized collective intelligence — anything from General Motors to the Internal Revenue Service — that someone wants to talk seriously to someone else about a problem. This last observation not only is an interesting theoretical one, but it also implies some significant opportunities to improve performance at the margin. If, indeed, courts are being used to get past unresponsive, incompetent, or indifferent clerks in

---

[6]I have discussed this process at length in my book *The Divorce Decision* (New York: McGraw-Hill, 1984).

the lower corporate or government bureaucracy, and if what plaintiffs really want is a serious conversation but not necessarily a serious lawsuit, then much is to be gained by responding to frustrated people with a little cheap accommodation and tender loving care rather than hardball, all-or-nothing litigation.

As late as the conclusion of World War II over 17 percent of Americans were farmers. By 1985 the farm population had dropped to 2.4 percent. Unlike our grandfathers who were born, lived, and died in a nation of small-town, self-reliant farmers and small entrepreneurs, we are increasingly a nation of city dwellers living under the power of others. For example, the investment decisions of anonymous corporate managers in a boardroom in New York can spell life or death for a manufacturing city like Richmond, Indiana, or McKeesport, Pennsylvania. Our children's education depends on public schools, and this is even more true as single-parent families and two-income families provide less parental guidance. Recreation depends on public facilities; health depends on hospitals, doctors, and government rules about insurance; the value of our property depends on zoning laws; and our incomes depend on government grants, subsidies, and tax breaks. We do not even die at home any more; we go to nursing homes for professional death management.

Today we have companies like American Express, MasterCard, and Visa that began by providing a convenience and have ended up with the near-monopoly of an utter necessity. Try sometime, for example, either to check into a hotel or rent a car without a valid credit card to vouch for the fact that you are an identifiable human being — even if you present a fistful of hundred-dollar bills and demonstrate a willingness to pay cash. When a person's credit card is cancelled, then, he loses his identity and will inevitably go to court to get it back. This is a completely new problem, which courts will probably handle because it is a problem that is not being handled elsewhere.

Big business is replacing small business — and often it is not even U.S. big business, but the big business of the Pacific Basin or Europe. In manufacturing, most consumer products — cars, appliances, drugs, and even housing — are made by distant giants. Small restaurants are being forced out by fast food chains; local stores are closed under the pressure of chain discounters; and local banks that were formerly controlled by local boards of directors are being gobbled up by statewide or even regional banks operated locally by indifferent strangers selected from a central management pool of hotshot kids with MBAs.

As the magnitude and breadth of our interdependence increases annually, we intensify our search for protection from impersonal and apparently uncontrollable forces like corporations, governments, and even runaway computers. People have found such shelter in the courts, which give them leverage against those with power and mitigate the caprice of major institutions. People turn to the courts both to widen their participation in a society increasingly dominated by experts like school administrators, welfare workers, and government regulators and to provide a buffer against all sorts of decisions that adversely affect their lives. When business plans to build a skunkworks in your neighborhood, you don't go to the board of directors 1,500 miles away but to your local court. Strangely enough, however, when a local zoning board serves up a heap of home cooking to a national company to prevent construction of a skunkworks, the company goes to court, hoping that the local judges will have more integrity than the local political establishment.

The rise of the courts as the United States' preeminent governing force is, then, a response to the exponential pace of technological change. The original eighteenth- and nineteenth-century design of our government is being strained, as it has been strained at times in the past. In the 1860s our response to strain was civil war; in the 1930s, we created federal and state administrative agencies; and since the 1960s, we have expanded the functions and power of the courts.

The shift in the center of political power can be seen most clearly in the shifting attitudes of the judges themselves. This is a phenomenon that is difficult to quantify because the ceremony and useful illusions that surround the judiciary make judges reluctant to give honest answers to investigators, even when there is credible assurance of anonymity. Judges, however, talk among themselves, and for the past thirteen years I have listened to what they have been saying. What I have heard discloses a marked change in attitude among judges.

A decade ago, and certainly two decades ago, when judges intruded themselves into the political process, it was with sincere reluctance; there was a widespread feeling among judges that most things of political importance should be sorted out by politicians and that courts should be politically active only on rare occasions when the political process was deadlocked. Today judges are much more willing to acknowledge their political roles, and this leads me to believe that courts will be expanding their political power at an accelerating pace.

Until the 1960s law schools taught that judges and lawyers were to extend existing law only in those cases where the existing law was inadequate. Furthermore, law schools taught that when law was extended in one area, the new rules should follow logically — almost inevitably — from established principles in other areas. In general, the law schools did not teach that judges were free to make up whatever rules pleased them. Respect for precedent — and through precedent, for stability and predictability — was taught as the preeminent goal of legal science, even at the expense of individual justice. Judges, in turn, were influenced by peer pressure to articulate their decisions in terms of precedent and natural law. Courts still made law, but at the same time judges did everything they could to disguise the fact that they were manufacturers rather than simple distributors of law. The dynamic tension between stability and change remained on the side of the former until the 1960s in the federal courts and the 1970s in most state courts.

Students try to please their teachers throughout their lives; therefore, the type of education that a professional class receives influences the actions of that class for a generation. When most of our judges were men and women educated in the 1930s and 1940s, the courts reflected the attitudes of the law schools of that earlier era. Indeed, in the late 1920s the Yale Law School had already pioneered a school of jurisprudence known as "legal realism," which taught that law strongly reflects the policy choices of the judges. The legal realism school was often caricatured as teaching that court decisions are the product of what the judges have for breakfast, but in the early days of legal realism there was widespread recognition among its originators that it was an extreme statement intentionally designed to point out but one of the many aspects of how courts work.

For three decades beginning in the early 1930s, legal realism had prominent followers in the major national law schools but remained outside the mainstream of legal education. At a school like the University of Virginia, even as late as 1965, legal realism was regarded by a majority of the faculty as an eccentricity.

The activism of the U.S. Supreme Court — beginning with the integration decision of 1954 and followed by wholesale federal judicial revision of state criminal law in the early 1960s and by federal judicial control of state laws governing birth control, censorship, government personnel firings, and civil rights in the middle 1960s — gave added credibility to Yale's legal realists. Even more important, both the faculty and students at the national law schools were enthusiastically in favor of the political results that the Supreme Court was achieving, which meant that legal realism slowly changed from being a critical tool into being a justification for what the Supreme Court was in fact doing. In order to defend the Court's results it became necessary to defend the court's process, and that meant teaching that judge-made law ought to reflect the policy choices of judges. This latter evolution of legal realism is what I was taught by such eminent Yale professors as Alexander Bickel and Charles Reich in the 1960s; but when I became a judge fifteen years ahead of my classmates, in 1973, I found few like-minded judges sitting on state court benches.

A frankly acknowledged, active political role for judges seemed perfectly natural to me; however, it did not seem perfectly natural to my older state-bench colleagues. This is not to say, of course, that my older colleagues were not politically active on occasion, but there was a reluctance to admit — even in the privacy of the judges' conference room — that the court was taking political bulls by their horns. Today there is no such reluctance.

The Supreme Court of the United States usually has accomplished its feats of judicial policymaking through interpretations of the vague clauses of the U.S. Constitution — particularly the due process and equal protection clauses of the fourteenth amendment. In the 1960s and early 1970s, when state courts felt called on to engage in similar policymaking at the state level, they usually repaired as well to the U.S. Constitution. That process, however, made their decisions vulnerable to reversal on appeal by the Supreme Court — the final authority on the Constitution. But by 1980 the state courts had learned to use vague clauses in their own state constitutions as vehicles for judicial lawmaking, and this technique made state court decisions almost invulnerable to troublesome meddling by the Supreme Court.

Whether the legal-realist defenders of the Supreme Court were (or are) right makes little difference: What's important is that by the 1970s the leaders of the legal profession no longer believed in, or at least no longer pretended to believe in, a sacred body of doctrine that had been revealed to judges over nine centuries. When this particular illusion went down the tubes, it took with it many of the forces favoring stability. Once the thesis of the legal realists that judges are simply powerful politicians was accepted as gospel — a situation that increasingly appears to be the case in all court systems — courts no longer felt bound by the rules of prior generations with which they disagreed. It was no longer necessary for judges to twist themselves out of shape in their opinions to show how a new rule flowed inevitably — and even logically — from older rules.

This whole phenomenon is of far more than academic interest to the practicing businessperson because it is at the heart of *ex post facto* lawmaking — a danger to which business is increasingly exposed in such areas as product liability, environmental torts, and personnel firings.[7] Earlier in this century when the courts waxed eloquent about "natural law," courts defended themselves against the charge of *ex post facto* lawmaking by maintaining that they were simply applying inherently reasonable principles to new situations. Litigants, they maintained, could not be surprised by new forms of liability that the courts might create because the litigants themselves could have divined the new principles as easily as the judges. In the post–legal-realist era, however, courts are content to overrule old law and replace it with new law that can bankrupt in a stroke a previously solvent firm. Now there is no longer even the pretense that litigants can figure out new rules for themselves, and with the disappearance of the old but useful illusion that courts divine new legal rules from a body of divinely ordained natural principles, many of the restraints that held retroactive civil lawmaking within tolerable bounds have disappeared.

A good example of the type of expectation-shattering litigation to which business is now exposed involves the theory of "comparable worth" in the private labor market. The women's advocates want someone to evaluate all the jobs in the economy in terms of their fatigue, danger, necessary education and training, and other factors such as security, working conditions, and the work's inherent interest. When women are paid less for performing jobs that are "comparable" to those of men, they want the wages to be comparable.

There are some dismal statistics that cause women who understand the subject to place legislation on "comparable worth" high on the political agenda. For example, the mean wage for women who work full-time is only 59 percent of the equivalent mean wage for men, and in married households where both husband and wife work full-time, the woman's wage on average amounts to only 34.7 percent of the family's earnings. In fact, a whole new class of poor

---

[7]I use the expression *"ex post facto"* here the way it would be used by businesspeople and not the way it would be used by lawyers, who would confine the use of *ex post facto* to criminal law and use "retroactive law" when talking about civil law.

is emerging in the United States — untrained divorced women with minor children. Women, who constitute 42 percent of the work force nationally, are concentrated in a small number of occupations, with low pay and limited opportunities.[8]

Furthermore, there is strong evidence that occupational segregation of women is increasing. In 1950, 62 percent of all clerical workers were women; by 1978 the figure had risen to 79 percent. Inevitably, therefore, pressure has developed to use political means to enhance the relative earning power of women because the free market for labor does not appear to be equating the value of women's services with those of men. Simply put, the women's advocates argue that women are systematically segregated into low-paying jobs where the number of women competing for those jobs keeps the wages low. Employers, on the other hand, argue that women are now free to compete on equal terms for almost any job and that market forces set wages. Women, employers argue, do not want to be traveling salespeople on commission, outdoor telephone repair persons, or automobile mechanics. As is usual in these types of matters, the truth probably lies somewhere in between.

Business, of course, is terrified of the concept of comparable worth because implementation in both business and government will cost an estimated $320 billion a year[9] and create a regulatory nightmare with constant, expensive litigation. What is of interest to us here, however, is not who has the better side of the comparable worth question but rather the different ways that the question can be settled.

It should hardly come as a surprise that Congress and the state legislatures can pass statutes requiring wages based on comparable

---

[8]Government studies show that in 1981 half of the 43 million women in the labor force were employed in only twenty-one occupations; secretary, bookkeeper, sales clerk, retail worker, cashier, waitress, registered nurse, elementary school teacher, private household worker, typist, nursing aide, sewer and stitcher, cook, receptionist, secondary school teacher, assembler, bank teller, building interior cleaner, hairdresser, cleaner and servant, and child-care worker.

[9]See N. Rothchild, "Toward Comparable Worth: The Minnesota Experience," 2 *Yale Law and Policy Review* 346, particularly note 31.

worth. In fact, this is what the state of Minnesota has done for all state workers, under a plan that calls for phasing in higher wages for women (although men are also affected) over several years. But Minnesota has not yet tampered with the private sector. What might come as a surprise to businesspeople, however, is that most of the serious advocates of comparable worth in the private sector have largely abandoned the legislative route. Instead, they place most of their faith in the willingness of courts to chip away at market wage rates through judicial decisions.

The mechanism for performing this latter service on a national basis is title VII of the Civil Rights Act of 1964. So far, however, the courts have interpreted title VII only to forbid discrimination on the basis of sex in wage rates when men and women are doing the same job. Except in a few fact-specific cases, title VII has not been interpreted to allow a comparison of wage rates between entirely different jobs, such as outside sewer cleaner and inside janitor. Nonetheless, it would be a short leap indeed from where we are now under title VII and its complementary statute, the Federal Equal Pay Act, to comparable worth.

Furthermore, the proponents of comparable worth frankly admit that their salvation will come from the courts and *not* from Congress. They want legislation, and they explicitly admit that this legislation can and should come from the courts. Here, for example, is what a young law student named Melinda P. Chandler wrote in a comment on comparable worth in the *Northwestern University Law Review* in 1980 (emphasis added):[10]

> The series of court cases in this area, restrictive and liberal in their interpretation of Title VII alike, are a challenge to Congress to rewrite sex discrimination legislation on a large-scale basis. *At the very least, these cases should be read as a challenge to the Supreme Court to ultimately resolve the ambiguity raised by commentators on the Bennett Amendment* [an amendment that limited antisex discrimination under title VII to instances that would qualify

---

[10]"Equal Pay for Comparable Work Value," 75 *Northwestern University Law Review* 914 (1980).

*under the Equal Pay Act] and to explicitly apply Title VII to all cases
of undercompensation due to job segregation, whether by race, religion,
sex or national origin.*

Obviously Chandler and the law review editors who approved
her piece are little impressed by traditional distinctions between legislative and judicial powers. She sees no impediment to the courts'
wholesale legislating of a complex and questionable economic policy. The paragraph I have just quoted shows that she looks on courts
as a superlegislature. Chandler's article is a handsome piece of legal
scholarship, and I use her paragraph to show that by 1980 even legal
ingénues and their mentors accepted as sound law that if you can't
get what you want from Congress, take another bite at the apple in
the courts.

Everyone in the process nowadays is quite candid about the
fact that judges have no reluctance, when it suits them, to interpret
a statute in a way that entirely confounds Congress' intent. Chandler sees no good reason why courts should not be free to pervert
title VII, notwithstanding that any honest reading of its legislative
history shows that title VII was never intended to do anything as
radical as mandate private-sector wages based on comparable
worth. And, perhaps to state the obvious, it makes a great deal of
difference from business' point of view whether Chandler ever
makes it to the Supreme Court of the United States!

Ms. Chandler's law review article is another example of a significant change in tone from yesteryear. In fact, we now appear to
have in the United States what sociologists call a lack of "attitude/
behavior congruence." Simply illustrated, that means that if you ask
the average American what she thinks of parliamentary democracy,
she will indicate her strong approval of that system. Yet whenever
the same American is confronted by a decision adverse to her interests that has emerged from the elected branches of government, she
will try to get that decision overturned in the courts.

State court judges consistently speak disparagingly (at least in private) of their state legislatures, and they are encouraged in their low esteem for legislators by popular sentiment. Few government officials receive more obloquy than state legislators, and the proof of that pudding is that every year more and more "appeals" are brought to the courts from the decisions of legislatures! For example, in 1976 the supreme court of New Jersey as much as ordered the New Jersey legislature to enact an income tax to support the state's public schools. Instead of being impeached, however, the supreme court justices of New Jersey emerged from the clash with New Jersey's legislature as national heroes! The new income tax meant that poor children — particularly black children living in property-tax-poor school districts — would get better educations.

Most humane people applauded the New Jersey court's result, and from an institutional point of view the decision was probably right even under its particular political circumstances. But the point is not whether the result was right or wrong but rather that when courts and legislatures clash today the courts come out the winners because they have popular opinion on their side. This encourages them, then, to challenge more and more decisions made by legislatures and governors.

It used to be that when a court rendered a decision offensive to legislators, the legislature would enact a statute obliterating the new court-made law. In fact, this is how things were thought to work in England and the United States for at least the past four hundred years, and it is probably the way that nine out of ten political science professors tell their students that things still work today. But contrary to accepted theory the opposite dynamic actually prevails now. Through our courts' ability to constitutionalize every imaginable issue, the courts have turned the process on its head and are in the business of overruling the decisions of legislatures. Courts still acquiesce in the legislative will on subjects that they don't care about, like intestate succession or the requirements for a valid deed, but when legislatures challenge courts on issues that interest the judges, the judges usually win.

If the new generation of judges shows less deference toward the other branches of government and appears more arrogant about its own capacity to govern, those flaws are not attributable to defects in its character or education. Neither Congress nor the state legislatures appear to have any serious inclination to overrule judge-made law, and in many regards the legislatures have abetted the shift in power away from themselves by delegating the hard decisions to the courts. For example, in the floor debate that surrounded the enactment of title VII of the Civil Rights Act (the legislation that conceivably allows court decisions on comparable worth) it was frankly admitted that Congress wasn't sure what the statute would do but that the courts would satisfactorily sort it out!

In my thirteen years on a state's highest court, only five of our court's decisions have been challenged legislatively, and in only one of them had we trotted out the big gun of constitutionalization.[11] What has happened is that in many areas of governing the other two branches have just given up and consigned the problems to the courts. Courts operate, however, in an entirely different way from either legislatures or administrative agencies, and one important part of the way they make law concerns the fact that decisional law is always made in the context of lawsuits. This means that courts are inherently backward-looking, and if new law is to be made, it must apply to facts that arose before the law was made. Thus, as courts take on more and more governing functions, business will increasingly be exposed to the hazards of retroactive lawmaking.

---

[11]One of these decisions was the legislature's partial restoration of employer immunity from suit by employees for work-related injuries after the court eroded that immunity; another abolished the maternal preference in child custody cases; another reestablished the right of teachers to paddle school children; and the last two involved taxes, including the constitutional amendment restoring less-than-market-value property assessment that I discussed in chapter 1. In twelve years, however, our court has decided well over 200 cases creating new general legal principles, and the other cases have gone unchallenged.

Chapter 4

Ex Post Facto Law

When businesspeople *are victimized by retroactive* law, they wonder where the Constitution is when they really need it. Their problem is that, like most Americans who are not lawyers, they do not realize that *ex post facto* law applies only in criminal cases, not civil cases.

The average American enjoys the happy but entirely unjustified belief that he or she is protected from all forms of *ex post facto* lawmaking. This particular widespread fantasy is founded on two narrow provisions of the Constitution of the United States, namely article 1, sections 9 and 10. Section 9 simply says, "No Bill of Attainder or *ex post facto* law shall be passed," and section 10, placing limits on the power of the states, says, "No state shall . . . pass any Bill of Attainder, *ex post facto* law, or law impairing the Obligation of Contracts." Although the term "*ex post facto* law" is often used synonymously with "retroactive law," the two are not the same.

The constitutional prohibition against *ex post facto* laws applies *only* to criminal law; it has not been applied to civil laws passed by the Congress or the state legislatures, and it certainly does not apply to judge-made, civil law. Indeed, courts have often struck down retroactive civil laws passed by Congress or state legislatures, but they have not based their decisions on the *ex post facto* law provisions of the U.S. Constitution. Rather, courts have based their decisions protecting us against retroactive civil lawmaking either on state constitutions or on the federal "due process" or "obligation of contracts" clauses. Whether, however, a particular retroactive civil law violates some nonspecific constitutional principle like "due process" is a hit-or-miss matter, and experience demonstrates that it is often miss.

Why is it that U.S. law faithfully honors principles against retroactive lawmaking in criminal law but can ignore them cavalierly in civil law? Part of the answer is that changes in the criminal law are entirely the responsibility of the legislature; although hundreds of years ago the courts developed criminal law along with the rest of the common law, they no longer do so. Because the greatest exposure to retroactive lawmaking occurs when courts themselves make law, the simple fact that criminal law is exclusively legislative reduces the hazard of retroactivity significantly. The rest of the answer may be counterintuitive but nonetheless accurate: In the criminal law nobody cares about the result.

Although victims understandably enjoy the emotion of revenge when a criminal is punished, no one benefits directly from criminal prosecutions because criminals have little capacity to make restitution for their misdeeds. In a general way prosecuting criminals discourages crime, but there is no public benefit other than incapacitating the criminal for a number of years attendant on any specific criminal prosecution. In fact, in the total legal system criminal law has a rather low priority: Criminals are usually prosecuted by young, underpaid, inexperienced assistant district attorneys, and they are usually defended by equally young, equally underpaid, and equally inexperienced public defenders.

Furthermore, because everyone fears being prosecuted for a crime that wasn't a crime when he committed it, we might say that "no *ex post facto* law" is the most important principle in criminal jurisprudence. In comparison to the personal security that comes from knowing that before anything we are doing can be called a crime, a legislature must give us advance notice, all other considerations, such as getting criminals off the street or exacting vengeance, pale. Occasionally we find that the federal courts are cavalier about *ex post facto* principles in white-collar prosecutions under the vague and open-ended federal conspiracy statutes, but with a few aberrations like federal conspiracy, it is generally conceded that the *ex post facto* prohibition in criminal law is strictly and literally honored more than perhaps any other single legal principle.[1] It is, then, this strict and literal application of the antiretroactivity principle to *criminal* prosecutions that lulls us into a false sense of security about our liability under quickly changing civil law. Although a person cannot be put in jail for a month under an *ex post facto* drunk driving statute, he can easily be bankrupted and lose everything that he worked a lifetime to accumulate as the result of a retroactive, judge-made, product liability decision!

On the civil side the jurisprudential principle that law should have only prospective application is but one of numerous competing principles that interweave to make up the total fabric of the law. Furthermore, unlike criminal law, powerful political constituencies care a great deal about the results reached in civil cases because lots of money is at stake. When people win civil cases, they walk away with something more valuable than vengeance — namely, money — and when people lose civil cases they often go bankrupt.

The very simplicity of the criminal law makes it easy to achieve firm, near absolute principles defining when a law has an *ex post facto* dimension. Concisely, before a person can be prosecuted for a

---

[1]When I was teaching in the People's Republic of China in 1984 I observed that one of the government's control devices among university students is its routine prosecution of young people for "thought crimes" that require no predefined overt act. From what I could gather from the English and U.S. students who spoke fluent Chinese and had spent a year or more at Fudan University, the government "disappeared" students — one wonders whether they were shot — for having bad attitudes. Because the type of attitude that got you "disappeared" had never been defined, there was an understandable sense of conservatism and conformity among the university community.

crime, the act of which he is accused must have been defined as a crime at the time he committed it. And it is an easy extension of this principle to conclude that both the penalty for the crime and the rules for prosecuting the defendant cannot be changed for that defendant after the crime has been committed. In the civil arena, however, the universe of possible transactions is so immense that it is not possible to draw hard and fast lines about what constitutes impermissible retroactive lawmaking.

For example, is a new tax law that changes the rules governing the rate at which owners of buildings can depreciate their buildings a retroactive law? Certainly it is not retroactive with regard to anyone who does not already own a building. But what about owners who have already built buildings and whose profit and loss projections were based on the old depreciation schedule? If, indeed, applying new depreciation schedules to old buildings is impermissible, then there would be few changes in the law that would be permissible. There is always some retroactive element in even the most forward-looking law changes. When Congress mandates higher average gas mileage for cars, the investment decisions of those who bought gasoline stations ten years ago are necessarily affected, and the new law has a retroactive dimension. Similarly, if the United States enters into a new trade treaty that reduces tariffs, the effect must be to lower demand for U.S. goods and adversely affect Americans who relied on the old tariff schedules when they built their plants.

On the civil law side, then, whether a particular law has a retroactive dimension is more a matter of degree than it is of kind. At the extremes almost everyone agrees on what is permissible and impermissible; thus, although Congress might change depreciation schedules effective during the tax year after passage, Congress would not change depreciation schedules and then seek to recapture the taxes saved in prior years when the more generous depreciation schedules were in effect. But in the area of trade agreements the relationship between new tariff rates and earlier reliance interests are so tenuous that principles against retroactive lawmaking are not a consideration. Treaty negotiators and Congress may take reliance interests into account in determining how quickly the new tariffs should become effective, but their actions in that regard will not be guided by principles governing retroactive lawmaking.

Among the three great centers of lawmaking power — legislatures, administrative agencies, and courts — it is the courts that create business' greatest exposure to retroactive civil law. Although both legislatures and administrative agencies can confound reliance interests by, for example, raising taxes or creating new environmental regulation, both legislatures and administrative agencies give careful consideration to the retroactive dimension of new rules and try to do as little violence as possible to legitimate reliance interests. New tax rates are often phased in over a number of years, and administrative agencies often insert "grandfather" exceptions in their environmental regulations to keep established but marginally profitable firms from going belly-up.

The irony of the hazard that the courts create by their own manufacture of retroactive law is that courts keep retroactive lawmaking by Congress, state legislatures, and administrative agencies within reasonable bounds. This phenomenon is partially related to criminal law: The typical vehicle for government regulation is a statute or agency rule that has at least a minor criminal penalty. But the courts are strict with the other branches about retroactive rules even when there are no criminal penalties. Courts probably would not allow Congress or the state legislatures to pass a law requiring the recall and free replacement of all tractors manufactured without roll bars, nor would the courts allow Congress to pass a tax whose measure is based on taxpayers' income three years before the tax's effective date. Which particular constitutional clause — due process or impairment of contracts, for example — courts would trot out to accomplish this feat I am not sure, but like Queen Victoria's chair that miraculously appeared whenever she decided to sit down, I know that something would be there when needed.[2]

The reason for the difference between what courts do themselves and what they allow legislatures and administrative agencies to do concerns the *ability* of the other branches to make rules with only prospective application. Because executives, legislators, and administrators can establish their own agendas, they can make law that applies only prospectively. Courts, on the other hand, *can't* make any law without some retroactive component because courts, by their very nature, are backward looking. It is the hope of a judgment based on *past* conduct that brings lawyers and litigants with new claims to court in the first place! But there is even a higher irony about courts themselves doing what they prohibit others from doing: Increasingly, the branches of government that *can* avoid retroactive lawmaking are unloading their own responsibilities onto the courts. When this occurs, of course, the hazard of retroactive lawmaking is correspondingly increased.

If, for example, the legislature passes a simple, unambiguous statute there is little chance of any retroactive application. But if the legislature passes a vague, poorly drafted statute that requires court interpretation, everyone may be surprised by the court's creative reading of the statutory language and then suffer when the court applies its own perverse conclusions about what the statute was intended to do to conduct that occurred between the passage of the statute and the court ruling. In such circumstances the court will assert, of course, that the statute was intended to do what the judges say it does from the statute's effective date. The truth, however, may be that strong-willed judges have used an ambiguous statute to achieve results that were never intended by the legislature, and this recurring phenomenon exacerbates the already difficult problems of statutory draftsmanship.

It must always be kept in mind that courts are powerful insti-

---

[2]For the reader who is interested in the variety of imaginative techniques that courts have used to attack retroactive civil laws, a good summary may be found in *American Jurisprudence 2d* (one of the two great legal encyclopedias) at volume 16A, "Constitutional Law," sections 661 to 701.

tutions and judges, like members of any other powerful institution, are jealous of their power. But the very nature of courts requires that the exercise of judicial power be in the context of adversarial cases, even if those cases occasionally arrive in court at the prompting of judges. No judge, regardless of his or her personal impatience, can decide to change the law in a particular way and issue an edict. Judges are constrained to wait until lawsuits arrive that present the issues they want to decide. Judges must govern through cases, and this simple operative principle of judicial power is at the heart of the courts' unpredictable manufacture of retroactive law.

Simply put, courts must be willing to award judgments based on conduct that was legal at the time it occurred if new cases supported by new legal theories are going to be brought to them on a regular basis. Because it is so expensive to go to court, private litigants will not bring cases to judges if they believe that favorable rulings will not apply to them. Litigation on the frontiers of the law is either subsidized by solvent clients who pay dearly for lawyers, or it is undertaken by lawyers for contingent fees. If, therefore, a change in the law will not benefit the litigant, neither the solvent client nor the contingent-fee lawyer can get paid, and both are out-of-pocket for the litigation expenses. For example, in the "unjustified firing" cases that are becoming a prominent hazard for business, the plaintiff employees simply want their jobs back or money judgments. They are not in court to make law so that someone else will get his or her job back or so that others will get money judgments in the future.

This returns us, then, to the phenomenon referred to in chapter 1 of the ever-growing lawyer population and the ever-growing number of lawsuits filed in the United States every year. The power of courts as lawmaking agencies is directly related both to the number and variety of cases brought to them for decision. The greater the number of lawsuits and the more creative the lawyers, the more extensive the power of courts becomes. Courts may accept or reject new legal theories, and in so doing they have the power to govern the United States. But as courts take on a progressively larger role in the governing process, business' exposure to retroactive lawmaking will correspondingly increase.

Although today's courts appear to be more cavalier about the retroactive dimension of their lawmaking than courts were at earlier times in Anglo-American history, judge-made law has always had a big retroactive component. This sinister side of the whole common law development process was obscured, however, by the comparatively slow pace of change in the first 800 years of Anglo-American legal history. Furthermore, as was indicated in chapter 3, until about the middle of this century there was a widespread belief among lawyers and law professors that our own legal system was simply a reflection of a divinely inspired scheme of natural law that has been revealed to judges over hundreds of years. When belief in natural law was replaced by "legal realism," many of the forces favoring stability lost their strength.

Courts, of course, are not the only source of retroactive liability. In terms of the likelihood of generating retroactive law, an administrative agency is somewhere between a legislature and a court. One of the things that extensive judicial review of administrative agency decisions has done is to make administrative agencies look and act like lower courts. When administrative agencies are engaged in court-like functions, such as adjudication, they too are likely to be cavalier about retroactive lawmaking. All agencies issue rules and regulations on which industry relies in the investment of large sums — as, for instance, in building nuclear power plants. Yet the agency can change its interpretation of its own rules and in so doing destroy millions of dollars' worth of investments. More to the point, however, when courts enter the administrative agency process there is an exponential increase in the likelihood of retroactive results.

For instance, there were 9,000 new federal regulations promulgated in fiscal 1981 that called for scrutiny of legal validity and for authoritative interpretation by a court. A firm that relies on an agency regulation when it is issued may be in big trouble five years later when an appeals court finally decides that the regulation was invalid from the outset. A court can invalidate an agency rule or regulation because it is inconsistent with what the court thinks is the statutory mandate. Furthermore, a court can decide to pervert the statutory mandate and substitute its conception of proper policy for the agency's conception.[3]

Part of the reason that business takes such a beating with regard to retroactive lawmaking in the courts is that business has a lock on the legislatures. Many of business' problems in the courts are directly related to the structure and organization of legislatures. (The entire next chapter is devoted to an examination of legislatures.) If, for example, product liability law could have been passed legislatively, it would have been magnificently forward looking because the judicial need to reward those who brought the cases to court would not have been present. But because no one thinks much about safety until he or she is injured, there has never been a political lobby any more potent than the trial lawyers actively trying to change product liability law.

The same dynamic of resort-to-court-because-the-legislatures-are-foreclosed holds true in the emerging law of "unjustified firing." Although I am more sanguine about the societywide effect of our products liability law than I am about the likely effects of a new,

---

[3]A good example of this process concerns the case of Vermont Yankee Power, a New England public utility that wanted to construct a nuclear power plant. The federal circuit court of appeals for the District of Columbia has an instinctive hatred of nuclear power, however, and blocked the Nuclear Regulatory Commission's authorization to construct the plant. The Supreme Court reversed, pointing out that such substitution of judgment was inappropriate — an entirely disingenuous admonition, since to my mind it stood only for the proposition that the Supreme Court likes nuclear power. *Aeschliman v. U.S. Nuclear Regulatory Commission*, 547 F.2d 622 (D.C. Cir. 1976), reversed by *Vermont Yankee Nuclear Power Corp. v. Natural Resources Defense Council*, 435 U.S. 519 (1978). See also *Natural Resources Defense Council v. U.S. Nuclear Regulatory Commission*, 685 F.2d 459 (D.C. Cir. 1982), reversed by *Baltimore Gas & Electric Co. v. Natural Resources Defense Council*, 462 U.S. 87 (1983).

nationwide common law of employment security, it might be instructive for a moment to play the devil's advocate here and point
out why, if it happens, employment security law will have a big
retroactive dimension. If, indeed, any changes in the current rules
governing at-will employment are to be made, the legislative structure that is described in chapter 5 makes the likelihood of such
changes coming from the legislatures vanishingly small. Business
may not "own" the legislatures, but business has a good long-term
lease! What lobby seeking greater employment security could conceivably overcome business's professional lobbying resources and
campaign contributions?

Certainly the labor unions aren't likely to push a general law of
job security because one of the biggest benefits that a worker gets
for his or her union dues is formal, ritualized job security. Unions
aren't in the business of helping either nonunionized workers or
managerial employees. Furthermore, fired workers are like accident
victims; few of us view ourselves as members of a class of "fired
workers" before we lose our jobs.

Ironically, retroactive court-made state decisional law on "unjustified firings" can be forestalled simply by passing a statute on
the subject. But business is successful in the legislative process not
because it can pass favorable statutes but rather because it can prevent *unfavorable* statutes from ever reaching the floor. In this regard
it is important to distinguish between defeating a bill and killing a
bill. Sophisticated lobbyists never want to defeat a bill by a record
vote; they want to kill a bill by silently burying it in committee. If,
indeed, business wanted to forestall court action on employment
tenure, it could initiate a pro-business statute on that subject and
get it placed high on the legislative agenda. Once on the agenda,
however, the bill would not long remain in the form in which it was
initially proposed by business. By the time business' original bill
had gone through cutting and pasting sessions in committee and
passed the amendment stage on the legislative floor, it would probably go a long way toward *creating* the very rights to employment
security that business initially wished to avoid. At the same time,
however, such a bill would completely protect business from the

retroactive effects of backward-looking court lawmaking. But who in business with an ounce of sense wants to make that trade? Business is better off taking its chances with the judges.

The effects of retroactive lawmaking, then, are like a tax that is exacted from business on those rare occasions when constituencies without a voice in the legislative process successfully appeal to the courts. Most of the time, however, when people lose in the legislature they also lose in the courts. Changing the system to allow greater opportunity for the unorganized to have access to the forward-looking legislative process rather than the retroactive court process might, indeed, reduce the occasions on which courts could justifiably make retroactive law, but from the point of view of business' overall political interests, the cure is deadly. If, therefore, courts are going to continue to be a viable balance to the legislative process (and in so doing reduce incentives to serious legislative reform that might jeopardize business' interests far more than they are currently jeopardized), then the price to be paid is exposure to retroactive court decisions.

Often, of course, there is sufficient pressure in a legislature so that business can't simply keep a bill on a particular subject bottled up in committee year after year. On those occasions business must enter into the give and take of politics, and if the antibusiness pressure is strong enough, perhaps the best that business can hope for is that legislators will find it difficult to achieve enough consensus to craft a detailed statute.

If there is pressure to do *something*, but no consensus about exactly what is to be done or how to do it, a legislature can react in one of three ways. First, it can pass a deliberately ambiguous statute that leaves the "what" and "how" either to the courts or to an administrative agency. This is a comparatively well-understood technique, and statutes of this sort at least give notice that both their method of implementation and their final effect are largely undefined until agencies and/or courts act. When such a bill is passed, business can protect itself by making "worst-case" assumptions, but business then has two more chances for a favorable outcome — first in the agency and then in the courts.

Legislatures may react to conflicting pressures in two other, and potentially more dangerous, ways. These involve the use of two cynical techniques, the *lex simulata* and the *lex imperfecta*, both of which would induce myocardial infarctions in eighth-grade civics text writers.[4] The *lex simulata* is simply a statute that looks like law but which, in fact, is purposely designed to do nothing. The *lex imperfecta* is a law that would do something were it not that a crucial piece of machinery — money, for example, — is missing.

Among the most notorious examples of *lex simulata* are elaborate reporting and disclosure requirements that in no way alter the substance of what is to be reported or disclosed. The Truth-in-Lending Act is a case in point; it did little beyond requiring borrowers to sign five pieces of paper that they don't read instead of one piece of paper that they don't read, and in so doing it increased substantially the cost of making loans.

In another permutation of the *lex simulata*, boards or agencies are formed to make recommendations to the legislature or to other boards or agencies. The political compromise that the *lex simulata* achieves is that proponents of substantive reform get a statute that appears to deter substantive abuses by exposing them to public scrutiny; the opponents of substantive reform, on the other hand, who understand the limited value of public scrutiny, are saddled with an annoyance—conceivably even an expensive annoyance—but they can still do business as usual.

Discussion of this subject is, perhaps, one of the rare occasions when I experience an almost uncontrollable sense of personal outrage. Experienced public officials understand, even if they seldom discuss it, that process reform is the final refuge of politics' greatest

---

[4]I am indebted for the invention of these two terms to Professor W. Michael Reisman of the Yale Law School who explains the techniques to which they refer with great precision as well as humor in *Folded Lies* (New York: Free Press, 1979).

scoundrels. Furthermore, the capacity of political low life to do damage through so-called process reform is directly related to the naïveté of sincere, college-educated, upper-middle-class voters who are easily manipulated by the press. Perhaps the high point of process reform in recent U.S. history was the period from 1974 to 1978 when the Vietnam war and related social unrest brought us political Armageddon.

Part of that political Armageddon was that scores of Democrats were elected to the House and Senate (as well as the state legislatures) from previously Republican areas. The election of those Democrats had almost nothing to do with their personal qualities; their prominence followed from that least incisive of all political exercises — turning the rascals out. And, unfortunately for those Democrats, the constituencies that elected them experienced no change whatsoever in their socioeconomic orientation; they were just as middle-class, agricultural, or socially conservative after Watergate as they were beforehand. Consequently, because the newly elected Democrats knew what was good for them, the last thing that they were going to do was act like Democrats; reelection absolutely demanded that they talk left but buy right, which is exactly what they did.

Thus it happened that the tactic that emerged for those who wanted to look like progressive reformers (talking left) while confounding no constituent's economic interests (buying right) was passionate commitment to apparently harmless process reform. Happily for Democrats with conservative constituencies, nobody with money to make campaign contributions who was not already dead against them gave a hot damn about the process. Perhaps because process is much easier to understand than economics, tax policy, cleaning out our ghettos, or defense spending, most of the college-educated junior executives, concerned housewives, and newspaper editors acted as if the process reformers had discovered Merlin's *Book of Magic*. Between 1974 and 1978 both Congress and the state legislatures gave us every imaginable form of political reporting requirement, access to government files, and reorganized the internal structure of Congress, state legislatures, and the political parties.[5]

In my experience process reformers are cowards or fools and frequently both. Their cowardice is exemplified by the fact that between 1974 and 1980 no serious attention was paid to substantive, ameliorative programs. Their stupidity is exemplified by one of the greatest achievements of the process reformers, the 1977 Foreign Corrupt Practices Act.[6] This most beautiful of all political actions told U.S. business that it is more important to export U.S. morality than it is to export U.S. goods; thus, in doing business with countries like Japan, Indonesia, or Saudi Arabia, where the kickback is a way of life, U.S. companies were forbidden to engage in bribery.

The *lex simulata* part of the Foreign Corrupt Practices Act was that U.S. companies doing business abroad could avoid its Rhadamanthine proscriptions simply by spinning off their foreign operations into separate foreign corporations. U.S. industrial workers had little notion of the act's ramifications at the time, although conservative estimates place the cost of lost contracts as a result of the act at over $2 billion a year.[7] The process reformers presented them-

---

[5]No action, however, was taken to cure the United States' urgent problems, such as the following representative list: increasing concentration of a dependent, jobless population in festering urban ghettos; high rates of inflation combined with high rates of unemployment; a progressive decline of high-wage U.S. manufacturing industry — steel, automobiles, appliances, coal mining; a movement toward national reliance on cheap imports, giving us by 1985 a yearly trade deficit with Japan of $30 billion; and finally, a decimation of the economic health of northeastern and northcentral cities by capital flights to low-tax, low-wage, nonunionized parts of the United States or even worse to foreign countries. Our inflation problem was finally ameliorated only by the worst depression since 1931 with national unemployment approaching 13 percent; the subsequent recovery was achieved through the greatest Keynsian infusion of borrowed money in history — approximately $220 billion a year.

[6]Public Law 95-213, title I, December 19, 1977.

[7]For a reference to the burdensome costs to U.S. business by the FCPA, see e.g., *Business Accounting and Foreign Trade Simplification Act: Joint Hearing on S.414 before the Subcommittee on International Finance and Monetary Policy and the Subcommittee on Securities of the Senate Committee on Banking, Housing, and Urban Affairs*, 98th Cong., 1st Sess. 33 (1983) (statement of Ambassador William Brock, U.S. trade representative). The U.S. State Department mournfully noted "that the Act hurts legitimate business trans-

selves as crusaders by riding an issue that was of little personal concern to ordinary voters in, say, Severna Park, Maryland, or Des Moines, Iowa.

If any U.S. company that had previously done business abroad wanted to continue to do business abroad without subjecting itself to U.S. prosecutions, it was required to spin off its foreign branches.[8] Foreign divisions of U.S. firms that had once proudly flown the U.S. flag and advanced U.S. interests (at least when all other commercial factors were equal) suddenly became French, German, Dutch, Korean, Taiwanese, or some other nationality. These subsidiaries, then, instead of remaining U.S. companies with patriotic responsibilities, became foreign companies with U.S. stockholders and no patriotic responsibilities other than paying Americans a quarterly dividend check.[9]

Sometimes process reform (as in the case of the Foreign Corrupt Practices Act) actually does something substantive, but more usually process reform is calculated to do little more than make a

---

actions by causing overcautiousness by American firms in trying to comply with the Act, confusion over what is a legitimate gift, problems related to local agent, difficulties in negotiating joint venture contracts; and heavy accounting expenses." *Id.* at 65 (statement by Denis Lamb, U.S. Department of State). The result of Congress's high-mindedness was "to encourage U.S. companies to concentrate their activity in geographic regions where there is relatively little risk of running afoul of the FCPA. One consequence is that U.S. firms are less likely than the European or Japanese competitors to enter the world's fastest growing export markets — developing countries." *Id.* at 79 (statement by Michael A. Samuels, U.S. Chamber of Commerce).

[8]15 U.S.C. sections 78a, 78m, 78dd-1, 78dd-2, 78ff(1983).

[9]It has been irritatingly difficult to find a source to cite for the proposition that a result of the Foreign Corrupt Practices Act's provisions has been for business to spin off its overseas holdings. U.S. businesses are not overly eager to make public the practice of divesting themselves of their overseas operations because a U.S. law was too hard to comply with. Yet the fact that this is occurring with alarming regularity is taken as an article of faith by those who are involved with the FCPA. Both Phillip Hinson, director of Middle East affairs of the international division of the U.S. Chamber of Commerce in Washington, D.C. and Professor William Eskridge of the University of Virginia School of Law admit to the seriousness of this problem. I first became aware of the problem during a conversation with former Senator Eugene McCarthy, an astute observer of such things and hardly either a notorious pro-business conservative or a man indifferent to the value of honesty either at home or abroad.

speech. Its classic manifestation, then, is the *lex simulata* that sets up boards, agencies, or commissions to receive reports, publicize substantive abuses, and recommend new legislation or agency orders. Disaster, however, occurs in the wonderland of *lex simulata* when judges are part of the constituency that wants substantive reform. Everyone gets burned when judges take a law that is intended only as a political speech and make it do something. When this happens, courts can be more dangerous to business than Congress or the legislatures themselves because whatever courts do to give teeth to *lex simulata* will have a retroactive dimension.

Several years ago, for example, at the height of the process reform movement the West Virginia legislature set up a board to review mine fatalities. The purpose of this board was to investigate the cause of all fatal accidents in coal mines and to recommend to the state director of mines rules that would prevent similar fatalities in the future. The entire scheme, however, was an exercise in *lex simulata* because the way the commission was staffed, with representatives from both industry and labor, ensured that nothing would happen. And, in fact, nothing ever did happen. The statute did not require the board to hold regular meetings; the board was not required to agree; and no mechanism was established to require majority and minority reports when the board did not agree.

In 1984, however, the United Mine Workers of America came to the West Virginia supreme court of appeals to get us to issue a writ of mandamus compelling the commission to meet soon after each accident and file prompt reports. The court issued the writ of mandamus, and overnight the commission turned from a pussycat into a tiger.[10] The final result, then, of *lex simulata* plus court intervention in the case of the mine fatality board was a situation far worse for industry than a more effective original statute would have been. When appellate judges want to be policymakers governing

---

[10]*United Mine Workers of America v. Scott,* 315 S.E.2d 614 (W. Va. 1984). The Court held that the board must "effectuate" its legislative mandate to protect coal miners by reviewing all mine fatalities and *issuing* rules and regulations to prevent such future accidents.

hot political subjects, statutes that are originally designed as dull-toothed *leges simulatae* are likely to be given sharp fangs.[11]

For the purposes of understanding retroactive lawmaking, the *lex imperfecta* is conceivably even more interesting than the *lex simulata* that we have just examined. As I mentioned earlier, in its classic form, the crucial missing piece of machinery for *lex imperfecta* is money, but there are variations, as we shall see. Perhaps the best example of the classic case, however, occurred during the 1970s when it was fashionable for state legislatures to pass "bills of rights" for mental patients and prisoners. Included in these catalogues of state humanitarian obligations were such entitlements as the right to appropriate treatment, the right to adequate living space, and the right to personal safety. The *imperfecta* part of these humane laws was that no money was appropriated to build facilities that would comply with the enunciated criteria or to hire staff capable of providing the care to which the statute said inmates were entitled.

A variation of this technique — and perhaps one that is of more urgent concern to business — occurred during the same period

---

[11]In fairness to courts, however, it should also be pointed out that sharp-toothed statutes are as likely to be defanged by judges as the reverse process I have been describing in the text. An example jumps quickly to mind from my own court in a case where a woman sued an insurance company under the West Virginia Unfair Trade Practices Act for inserting into her file a statement that she was associated with the Mafia. The Unfair Trade Practices Act makes it illegal to insert false material that disparages a person's credit standing in a business file. Nonetheless, in spite of the statute's apparently absolute language, our court held that all of the common law exceptions concerning "privileged communication" that have grown up in the law of libel and slander apply to the sections of the Unfair Trade Practices Act that prohibit the dissemination of false credit information. Recovery, then, became limited to cases where the false material was inserted in a file either with knowledge that it was false or with reckless and willful disregard of its possible falsity. Our reasoning in this regard was that the orderly transaction of business requires the exchange and storage of credit information and that creating a cause of action for damages whenever information inserted in a file in good faith turns out to be false has such a chilling effect on legitimate business information gathering that the legislature could not have intended such a result. *Mutafis v. Erie Insurance Exchange*, 328 S.E.2d 675 (W. Va. 1985).

when states established human rights commissions on a *lex imperfecta* basis. State statutes guaranteed access to housing, education, employment, and public accommodations without regard to race, creed, national origin, age, or sex, yet the powers of the human rights commissions, which were expected to enforce these guarantees, were limited to fact-finding, mediation, and ordering the person or firm who so discriminated to stop doing so. The state human rights commissions were notoriously understaffed and underpaid, while the enforcement procedures were expensive and time consuming because decisions could be appealed to several layers of courts.

Most of the time the *lex imperfecta* achieves its intended purposes — namely, to make a fine-sounding speech but do nothing. Occasionally, however, such imperfect statutes are used by Archimedes-like judges as fulcrums for big lawmaking levers. In the case of inmates' bills of rights, lawyers representing inmates went to state courts to enforce the rights. Frequently the courts responded by ruling that when the legislature enacted standards for the treatment of inmates, the legislature by implication enacted an entitlement to the money necessary to meet the standards. From a humanitarian perspective it is difficult to quarrel with those decisions, but the ultimate retroactive effect was to direct money away from existing programs on which many had relied and put it into hospitals or prisons. Efforts were also made to recover tort damages from either the state governments themselves or from individual administrators based on claims grounded in violation of the inmates' bills of rights. Although most of these claims were unsuccessful, the plaintiffs came close enough to winning to put the fear of God into wardens and hospital administrators.

Similarly, in some places the courts have responded to the *lex imperfecta* design of state human rights commissions by giving them powers that greatly exceed the original legislative grant. In New Jersey, for example, the state supreme court held that the human rights commission had *implied* power to award money damages to complainants in discrimination cases in addition to its authority to mediate and enter cease and desist orders. The result, of course, was retroactive lawmaking; discriminators who had expected nothing but speeches and some protracted litigation suddenly were stuck with money judgments for actions taken long before the New Jersey supreme court gave the commission power to make such awards.

One conclusion that should emerge from our analysis so far is that the more we rely on courts to moderate, temper, or otherwise annul adverse decisions made elsewhere in society, the greater our exposure to retroactive lawmaking. It is not that courts are the only lawmaking institution that makes rules that punish past actions; rather, it is that the retroactive dimension of new rules can be dealt with more forthrightly when issues are before either legislatures or administrative agencies. As the governing role of courts expands, business' exposure to retroactive lawmaking will correspondingly increase. An understanding of the dynamics of the process leads to two practical conclusions from business' point of view: First, retroactive lawmaking is a threat against which everyone should insure; and second, vague and undefined statutes are often more dangerous from business' point of view than more specific and yet ostensibly more unfavorable ones.

Every businessperson should always assume that many of the things that he or she is currently doing could result in heavy liability regardless of the current state of the law. At the simplest level, most states currently have law that holds, for example, that children's recreational devices — swings, seesaws, sliding boards, etc. — are not inherently dangerous. Therefore, if a child injures himself on such a device that is in good repair, there should be no liability. Nonetheless, the owner of an apartment complex where there is a playground is an idiot to rely on such law; if a child is seriously injured, a court will figure out some way to dip into the owner's pocket to take care of the child. Insurance against this hazard — i.e., the judicial hazard, not the playground hazard — is entirely in order. Similarly, although in most places the workers' compensation laws provide employers immunity from suits by employees for work-related accidents, that law is always being tested, and since omnibus liability insurance to protect against employee suits in excess of workers' compensation is cheap, it should always be bought.

Some changes in law, such as new but retroactive rules on employee firing, are difficult to insure against. The fact, however, that we can't insure against every horrible thing that courts might do to us does not mean that we shouldn't insure against as many as possible. Usually the law changes that carry the really big price tags occur in torts, and it is possible to insure against almost all forms of tort liability, even liability for torts that haven't been thought up yet. In unlawful discharge cases, for example, it is possible to insure against liability for punitive damages for "intentional infliction of emotional distress" under numerous omnibus excess liability policies that are on the market. In all respects, then, caution is the watchword. A businessperson's reliance on the current state of decisional law should always be tempered by a healthy skepticism; wherever possible (as, for instance, in firing cases) it is cheaper to settle with potential litigants than to rely on favorable law that is on the edge of a quickly changing frontier. Rule one: Never be the test case!

Similarly, when business is involved in the legislative process, it is often smarter to trade some substantive provisions in a bill for definiteness, rather than to rely on the usually benign character of either *lex simulata* or *lex imperfecta*. In this regard, many regulatory schemes that ostensibly entrust enforcement to an administrative agency (like, say, the National Labor Relations Board) could become nightmares for business if the courts ever allowed "private causes of action" grounded on the basic statute.[12] Often in the area of *lex*

---

[12]It is difficult to give a thumbnail sketch of the terrors of private causes of action, but it's worth a try. In many areas of economic regulation either Congress or a legislature establishes a policy and leaves its enforcement exclusively to an administrative agency like the National Labor Relations Board. The agency is usually somewhat incompetent, which means that there is much slack in enforcement. In other areas of economic regulation, however, Congress or a legislature establishes economic policy and then allows any individual who is injured by a violation of the policy to sue in state or federal court. Some statutes are explicit about which system of enforcement is intended, while others are not. When a court decides that an agency is too incompetent to enforce a statute, it may simply create a

imperfecta, when appropriate funding is not provided for regulatory agencies, courts will allow alternative private enforcement through private damage suits to rectify the balance. Better, then, to get a specific provision in the statute forbidding private causes of action, even if it costs concessions over funding levels, than to leave the subject open-ended. Today's courts, no matter how sympathetic they may be to business, will be replaced by tomorrow's courts, and open-ended statutes are a continuing invitation to judicial activism.

As a businessperson I always found that lawyers are the world's greatest deal-killers; they are so conservative that if one took too seriously their dire predictions about the potential legal problems of any given deal, no one would ever sign a contract or make a dime. Yet the natural conservatism of lawyers is entirely justified whenever they are discussing possible exposure to retroactive lawmaking. At least in this one area, it seems to me that the most technically oriented, mechanically minded lawyers should be listened to very carefully; their natural pessimism about courts and the stability of the law is well justified.

---

private cause of action and allow individuals, with the help of the courts, to enforce the statute themselves. Usually, however, this arrangement was not part of the politically bargained-for arrangement intended by the legislature.

Chapter 5

The Legislature:
Business' Favorite Forum

There is nothing about the courts themselves, except perhaps their reputation for integrity, that explains why they have been chosen as the repository for an increasing share of political power. Courts have very small supporting staffs, which makes it difficult for them to enforce or administer their orders; courts are composed exclusively of lawyers and secretaries, which means that judges and their helpers do not have significant internal expertise in science, economics, or management; and courts have such elaborate formal procedures surrounding the presentation of information that they are usually less well informed than other government agencies. The political power of courts, therefore, cannot be understood simply by looking at courts. Rather, courts can be understood only in relation to the structural rigidities, imperfections, incompetence, and even venality of other government power centers, particularly the legislative branch and the administrative agencies.

One of the initial points made in chapter 4 was that courts accrue power largely because there is no consensus about whether, how, or when to deny them power. Business' adversaries want the courts to do a number of things for them that they despair of achieving through Congress or the state legislatures, while business itself wants the courts to protect business from administrative agencies, tax-hungry states, and rapacious politicians. Thus it comes to pass that whenever courts do something that seriously offends business — like creating products liability law or establishing new rights for at-will employees — the "liberal" side, for want of a better word, of the political spectrum manages to hold the line in Congress and in the legislatures to prevent legislative reaction. Similarly, when the courts take action favorable to business — such as overruling administrative agency decisions about environmental regulations or determining that there is no private cause of action in the courts for the victims of unfair labor practices — the "conservative" side is able to forestall legislative reaction.

The purpose of this chapter and the next is to give the business reader a sense of the futility of devoting any significant resources to pie-in-the-sky schemes to return the courts to a less prominent place in national and state affairs. The work that the courts now do is unlikely to be absorbed by any other existing political instrumentality. As chapters 5 and 6 explain, the proper approach is not to attempt to gut the courts but rather to attempt to make them work more smoothly, more rationally, and more beneficially for business.

Back in the eighth grade we were all taught that legislatures make the laws, executives execute the laws, and courts interpret the laws. This tripartite division of responsibility implies, then, that a legislature is in business to pass new laws and modify old ones. Unfortunately, however, the eighth-grade civics model bears but a tenuous relation to reality. Legislatures are not designed to pass laws at all; rather, legislatures are designed to prevent laws from being passed.[1] Furthermore, it is generally a good idea that most

---

[1] During the 1985 legislative session of the New York state legislature, 14,895 bills were introduced from January to September. The members of the senate introduced 6,766 bills, 1,675 of which the senate passed. Of this 1,675, 711 also passed the general assembly. The members of the general assembly introduced 8,129 bills, 1,183 of which the general assembly passed. Of this 1,183, 359 also passed the senate. Of the 1,060 that passed both houses, the governor vetoed 148 and signed 912 into law.

legislation die a quiet death at the bottom of some obscure subcommittee's agenda because most of the laws proposed in any legislature go beyond benign stupidity to enter the land of theft and skulduggery with the commonwealth as intended victim.

Both in Washington and in many state capitals legislatures are housed in buildings of Greco-Roman designs. The architecture of legislatures, however, conveys a false historical message. Legislatures are not patterned after the classical democracies of antiquity, nor are they a modern variation of an ancient, classical theme. Congress and the state legislatures are feudal institutions in every sense of the word; they enjoy an unbroken historical evolution from their embryonic period during the reign of John (1199–1216), through the inclusion of a lower house (House of Commons) in the reign of Edward III (1327–1377), until they assumed roughly their modern form at the accession of William III (1689).

The early parliaments were explicit about the fact that their primary purpose was to prevent the executive and his minions from changing the customary organization of society: In other words, they said outright "No new laws!" In that static age, technology alone dictated that government could achieve little improvement for the populace as a whole. People were primarily concerned with avoiding new taxes, avoiding changes in the laws governing land tenure, and preventing onerous calls to military service. In fact the motto and war cry of the priests and barons who mobbed at Runnymede to extort the Great Charter from John in 1215 was "*Nolumus leges anglicae mutare*," traditionally translated as "The laws of England shall never change!" And this was hardly a political position that died and was buried in the Middle Ages; well into the nineteenth century references to *nolumus leges* may be found in the written records of the British Parliament. Parliaments, then, were originally designed to be intensely protective and conservative institutions.

It would appear at first glance that the twentieth-century United States has little in common with medieval, agrarian England or even the England of William III. Slightly closer scrutiny will disclose, however, at least as many similarities as there are differences, and one striking similarity remains: Whoever controls the machinery of government controls the distribution of wealth. A remarkably large portion of the bills introduced into any legislature today are designed as they were in medieval England — either to realign wealth positions among different groups or to redistribute wealth from the commonweal as a whole to the coffers of some particular interest group. The Civil Rights Act of 1964 is an example of the realignment of wealth and power between blacks and whites, while the oil depletion allowance is an example of redistribution of wealth from the commonweal to a particular interest group. Both the Civil Rights Act and the oil depletion allowance are striking examples of the process, but every legislature is confronted annually with a host of more humble petitions, most of which fail to pass.

When I was in the state legislature, the paradigmatic special interest bill was an apparently harmless proposal to require all plumbers to be licensed by the state. Ostensibly the bill's purpose was to assure consumers that their plumbers would be competent — a scheme that we currently use for doctors, lawyers, architects, engineers, and even barbers. In fact, of course, the plumbers' licensing bill was nothing but an attempt to get the state to limit output and in so doing raise prices. The particular incarnation of the bill on which I voted "grandfathered" in just about everyone who had ever stood within twenty feet of an overflowing commode with wrench in hand and made that person a licensed plumber without further ado. With regard to all others who would thereafter be allowed to hold themselves out as pipers-of-water-for-hire, however, it exacted a level of training that was about the equivalent of a degree in mechanical engineering from M.I.T. Many states have such legislation.

There is a monumental difference between doctors and lawyers on the one hand and plumbers on the other. Doctors and lawyers are dealing with an inaccessible body of knowledge, and doctors, at least, are dealing as well with inherently dangerous instrumentalities, such as drugs, x-rays, and sharp knives. If your doctor is incompetent, that fact may not dawn on you until you drop over the precipice from this life into the next; if your lawyer is incompetent, you may not discover the fact until you bid your family and friends a fond farewell to pull five to eighteen. If architects and engineers are incompetent, buildings tumble and fatalities ensue. But if your plumber is incompetent, the worst thing that can happen is that your toilet overflows or some pipe comes apart. There is no more point in regulating plumbers than there is in regulating television repairmen, roofers, chimney sweeps, or restaurant cooks. The difference between these latter purveyors of services and plumbers is entirely political; plumbers are organized into a craft guild that allows collective political action, while the others are not.

The plumbers are not the only organized interest group that descends on legislatures in an attempt to "get theirs." Although few of us ever notice it because it is so commonplace, U.S. society is characterized by a latticework of interest-group special privileges that legislatures have awarded, for one political reason or another, by statutory enactment. As with the plumbers' licensing bill it is always argued that there is some social justification for special treatment, and in many cases there is. There is a certain equity in giving coal miners special compensation for miners' black lung, and there is an educational value in allowing books and magazines to be sent through the mail for next to nothing. As a writer with a lot of neighbors who are coal miners, these are among my favorite special privileges.

Nonetheless, the biggest thing that most special privileges have going for them is raw political power. The unbeliever can try these on for size: The federal labor laws provide protection for industrial employees but exclude domestics, agricultural workers, and government employees. Bulk mailers can send heavy junk for less than a housewife can send a postcard; homeowners can deduct interest on their mortgage payments from taxable income, while apartment dwellers cannot deduct any part of their rent; industries hit by strikes receive no government aid, while striking workers get food stamps and occasionally unemployment compensation; businesspeople can deduct from taxable income personal cars, airplanes, and thinly disguised vacation travel, while factory workers pay tax on every cent of income; welfare recipients get a subsistence dole, while minimum wage employees receive barely more for a forty-hour week; and railroad employees may sue their employers in federal court for full damages for work-related injuries, while airline and truck workers must recover under state workers' compensation.

The stark recognition that most of what goes on in legislatures rises no higher than attempts by interest groups to use political muscle to extort preferential economic treatment for themselves places the negative bias of a legislature in an entirely new light. Suddenly the eighth-grade civics model is turned on its head; we no longer want a legislature hell-bent on passing new laws but rather a medieval parliament hell-bent on keeping new laws from being passed.

Unfortunately for proponents of a "truth in politics" policy, very few legislators have been returned to office on a platform that promised that they would go to Washington or the state capitol and do nothing. The reason is that when the average voter thinks of a legislature, she focuses either on what the legislature could do for her specifically or what it could do for society generally by passing "general interest" legislation. But it is a sorry fact of life that legislation that helps all of us without hurting anyone is almost unheard of in the real world. Much of the legislative process is a zero-sum game where politics determines the winners and losers. The tacit social agreement that the conscious design of a legislature reflects is that a zero-sum game isn't worth playing.

Most businesspeople who have had experience lobbying in Congress or a state legislature enjoy a cheerful cynicism about the legislative process as a whole. In the grand scheme of things, the lion's share of business lobbying is defensive; lobbyists work, for example, to prevent higher business taxes, to defeat new regulatory schemes, or to emasculate proposed pro-tenant amendments to existing landlord and tenant law. Like everyone else, however, business occasionally wants to initiate favorable legislation, and when business does, it is as much the victim of the legislative process' inherent inertia as anyone else. The difference, however, between business and most other groups who come to legislatures as supplicants is that business usually retains its sense of humor about the process.

Unlike other lobbyists, business lobbyists seldom argue that they have a *moral* right to new, favorable legislation. In general, business is not frustrated and enraged at the legislative process because, of the three branches of government, business achieves its greatest power in the legislature. When businesspeople become outraged over the legislative process, it is always because of something that the legislature has done; it is never because legislatures have a natural tendency to do nothing. Adam Smith had the first handle on legislative dynamics when he observed that mankind can tolerate a great deal of injustice but only a small amount of uncertainty. No change is usually good for business.[2]

In my experience business lobbyists are nice folks to have around because they don't behave ungraciously and they always have lush expense accounts that allow for opulent entertainment. Other lobbyists — the environmentalists or those pushing civil rights, for example — are not nearly as amusing and, because they have little money, certainly are not as entertaining. Also, lobbyists for public interest causes who lack the money to play the game in a gentlemanly manner often share a number of downright unamusing characteristics, such as a proclivity to stick their fingers in your face and rely on their moral claims to favorable legislation. Business, on the other hand, always operates in a low-key, professional way. Business does not picket the capitol, set up photographic displays in the lobby, or camp in your office in an effort to prove that you are out of touch with your constituents and indifferent to desperate public need because you fail to support a particular legislative pro-

---

[2]The Pennsylvania chamber of commerce estimates that in the typical legislative session 3,500 to 4,000 bills are introduced. On average 200 to 300 are of interest to business, and of these 20 to 30, they predict, will have a substantial negative effect on business.

gram. Instead, business just tries to show how particular legislation will enhance the overall health of the economy — particularly jobs, investment, and the attraction of high-wage industry. If those arguments are unpersuasive, business simply bribes you.

Businesspeople, however, must resist their natural tendency to impute the equanimity with which they view the whole legislative process to everyone else in society. Most nonbusiness entities that go to Congress or the state legislatures for new legislation believe intensely that they have a *moral* right to such new legislation. The women who understand the theory of comparable worth attribute any opposition to legislating higher, "comparable" wages for women to male chauvinist piggery: To them comparable worth is so inherently right morally that there can be no motivation but a corrupt one for opposition.

Business' traditional response to judicial activism is to argue that the things the courts are doing should be "left to the legislature." By saying this, business rises to no higher grasp of political theory than Ms. Chandler from chapter 3, who suggested that the proper place for legislating wages based on "comparable worth" is the courts. Both business and Chandler work backward from the result that they want to achieve to some conclusion about the appropriate forum for making the decision — namely, the forum most likely to give them what they want. The truth of the matter, then, is that because business is quite happy in a society where there is little legal change, business gets a perfect result in the legislative process more often than it does anywhere else in government. Business' adversaries, on the other hand, have the exact opposite experience.

Business' happy relationship with the legislative branch is the product of two distinct factors: First, the size and organization of Congress or a state legislature produce an almost insurmountable inertia; second, business has money, and legislatures are easy to bribe. Given these two institutional qualities, it should hardly be surprising that all the nonbusiness constituencies find legislatures obstacles to achieving their vision of social justice and turn to the courts. Why would ecologists, women's advocates, residential tenants, or unemployed members of minority groups pump up a branch of government — the legislature — that is institutionally designed either to do nothing or to be their active enemy? They use the rapier of the courts against the cudgel of the legislatures.

We can explore for a moment the two qualities that make legislatures the natural habitat of business, but in reverse order starting with the most incisive of all political techniques — bribery. Nowadays the paper poke of long green delivered to the committee chairman's office is out of fashion. The Justice Department's ferreting out of bribery and corruption at the state level in the last twenty years has severely reduced everyone's sense of humor about explicit payoffs. Illegal bribery is out of fashion; but it has been replaced by legal bribery that everyone reports with methodical care to a plethora of boards, election officials, and commissions.

For example, Representative Henson Moore of Louisiana had $332,000 left over when he won reelection in 1982 by 87 percent of the vote, and he continued to raise money at an unflagging pace, adding another $273,000 through 1983 and the first six months of 1984. Representative Dan Rostenkowski of Illinois (one of Congress' most powerful committee chairmen) raised $519,000 for the 1982 campaign, although he ran nearly unopposed, and Rostenkowski raised another $168,000 in 1983. Rostenkowski is the chairman of the tax-writing Ways and Means Committee, whose members, along with those of the parallel Senate Finance Committee, have the easiest time obtaining donations, since they are in the best position to do specific money favors for specific industries.[3]

Campaign contributions, however, are largely limited to use in campaigns. There is always some leakage — such as putting your wife on the campaign payroll or paying your foreign travel expenses from campaign funds ostensibly to generate good publicity — but

---

[3]I am indebted here and throughout much of the rest of this chapter to an incomparable piece of investigative reporting by Gregg Easterbrook, "What's Wrong with Congress?," *The Atlantic Monthly* (December 1984).

leakage has limited potential. Fortunately for interest groups wishing to make cash payoffs to legislators, there is no need to go exclusively along the campaign contribution route; influence buyers can simply pay an honorarium for a speech — money that goes straight into a legislator's pocket. In fact, eleven senators earned more in 1983 from speaking fees than from their salaries. Richard Lugar of Indiana netted $129,065 (after contributions to charity) from honoraria; Robert Dole, the Senate's new majority leader, netted $106,000; and twenty-one senators took in more than $50,000.

Corporations pushing a bill that limits product liability paid $34,000 to Senator Paul Laxalt, $40,350 to Senator Orin Hatch, and $26,250 to Senator Bob Kasten from 1981 through 1983. These latter numbers do not inspire confidence that if the whole subject of products liability had been "left to the legislature" anything much would have happened. Now that the courts have created extensive products liability law, business must work like beavers trying to keep it under control. But what chance would products liability have ever had to get off the ground in the legislative process in the first place? How many injured accident victims would have paid senators or state legislators to make speeches? Typically people who are injured in products liability cases are poor working stiffs; they hardly constitute a tightly knit, well-organized, powerful lobby. Even the products liability lawyers who have a substantial and continuing economic interest in successful tort recoveries cannot match the type of money I have just listed, particularly since there is more where that came from.

It is easy to comb through the files of campaign contributions and reported outside income to come up with some egregious examples of legal bribery. Dwelling on these examples, however, probably gives a false impression. In fact, in my own experience, few legislators — either state or federal — profit financially from government service beyond their salaries and proper perquisites. Some of the most notable exceptions to this rule are lawyers who are also state legislators because being a powerful legislative committee chairman inevitably helps anyone practicing law. It is remarkable, however, how many lawyer/legislators turn down opportunities to represent clients who want to pay for legal services but buy legislative services. Contrary to all of the "Best Congress Money Can Buy" stories in the popular press, what is noticeable in both Congress and the state legislatures is not how much bribery there is, but rather how little. Any student of U.S. history must be struck by the difference between the overall level of corruption in our society in 1986 compared to 1886. As we have matured we have also become marginally more honest.

Therefore, the most prominent legislative corruption does not take the form of personal bribery but simply of politics as usual. It is estimated, for example, that only about 21 percent of all adults are regular readers of daily newspapers. This fact alone bespeaks a society that is largely indifferent to politics. It also means that for approximately 79 percent of the population eligible to vote, information comes primarily from the television and radio. In a society in which politics is a matter of indifference to most people and television provides the bulk of all information, elected office has become a commodity for barter and sale through slick advertising. In addition, in many places elections can still be decided through the age-old technique of vote buying by well-organized political machines. This latter undertaking is not done as crassly as it once was, but votes can still be bought perfectly legally and very effectively.

Usually vote buying is now accomplished by the hiring of cars and drivers or the hiring of outside poll workers. When a political machine pays a man $500 to drive his friends and neighbors to the polls or just to work outside the polls for a day, it is assumed that the hired worker will first drive the ten persons in his or her family whose votes he controls. If you want to steal an election, you always work through honest people; no one but an idiot would hire poll workers who lacked the integrity to guarantee delivery of at least ten favorable votes in return for the $500.[4]

---

[4]Once upon a time in Harrison County, West Virginia, I watched an opponent of John D. Rockefeller line up every first-class precinct worker in the county by the Saturday night before the Tuesday election for governor. But by the following Monday night every worker had been bought out from under him by the Rockefeller organization at twice the going rate!

The biggest problem for both voters and legislators in the legislative process is how to handle legitimate campaign contributions. Election campaigns are expensive, and the people who can contribute money are the people who have money. In West Virginia, for example, the salary of a state senator is $6,500 a year; yet a contested primary campaign for the democratic nomination to the state senate typically costs between $20,000 and $60,000. Contested congressional races in West Virginia, a low-budget state, have now reached the $200,000 level, and in 1984 John D. Rockefeller IV spent over $11 million to be elected to the United States Senate. Obviously, for an ordinary politician to take on John D. Rockefeller IV requires a few friends with money! Query: Are contributions made by friends with money to a campaign to beat Rockefeller considered bribery? Maybe not, but $11 million in campaign contributions by businesspeople who employ hundreds of female workers might look that way to a woman secretary who wonders why so little has been done about comparable worth.

The bottom line in all this is that even if we imagine a legislative branch composed entirely of persons of consummate integrity, legitimate needs to win elections will always give constituents with money an edge on access to legislators and for that reason an edge on results. The bribery that really counts in a legislature is not the occasional crass payoff, disguised as it may be as an honorarium or legal fee, but rather legitimate campaign contributions to meet real and not imagined campaign expenses. All legislators must be ready every two, four, or six years, depending on the term, to fend off challengers. From personal experience I can testify that raising money is the most difficult part of any political campaign. The traditional campaign activities — traveling, speaking, shaking hands, and eating rubber chicken — are all surpassingly easy and pleasant in comparison to fund-raising. In politics, as in business, the ability to raise large sums of money separates the sheep from the goats.

Ironically, all the things that we associate with a political campaign — speeches, factory gate handshaking, meetings with organizational leaders — are increasingly peripheral, defensive activities. The larger a legislator's constituency — both in terms of numbers of voters and geographical size — the more success in politics depends on media. Today the heavy artillery in politics consists of television, radio, and direct mail. Of course the longer a person has been an incumbent, the less he or she needs expensive media to retain a seat because of years of accumulated personal contacts. Yet even strong incumbents must be willing to spend at least a third of what a serious challenger is willing to spend if they expect to sleep well during the campaign.

Although few legislators of my acquaintance are personally corrupt, all of them like their jobs. Talented legislators can often earn five times their legislative salaries practicing law or going back into business. But the pressure on untalented legislators is overwhelming; if untalented legislators lose their jobs, they not only suffer loss of personal status and interesting work but they face acute economic hardship as well. The secret, then, of successful legislative lobbying involves raising large sums of money quickly and with minimum effort on the part of the legislator whom the lobbyist offers to help. Such a creature develops a reputation in Congress or a state legislature as a valuable friend, and this guarantees the lobbyist in question instant access to almost every legislator and, as a result of access, favorable action on most issues.

In the legislative process the power of money and organized interest groups is enhanced by low voter turnouts. In a majority of U.S. legislative districts there is one dominant party, which means that elections are won in primary elections and not general elections. Typically, in an off-year primary election, 22 percent of the vote turns out. If the dominant party is the Republican party, and that party outnumbers the Democrats six to four, then the election will be decided by 60 percent of 22 percent, or 13.5 percent of the total eligible vote. That means that with 6.8 percent of the total vote a candidate wins. In a primary election in a presidential year about 36 percent of the vote will turn out, which increases in a general election to over 60 percent. As a general rule it can probably be said that the lower the voter turnout, the more important the bought vote and organized interest groups like teachers and labor become; the higher the voter turnout, the more important slick media campaigns become because as the voter turnout gets larger, the proportion of directly interested, knowledgeable voters becomes smaller.

The mechanics of election campaigns dictates that the two groups that legislators must always please are organized constituent interest groups in their districts — like labor and teachers — and people with money. It makes little difference what challengers say during campaigns when they are underdogs taking on incumbents. The rules that apply to successful challengers no longer apply to the same challengers once they are incumbents. Challengers must rally the discontented by attacking the character or record of those in office and offering new programs or new approaches. But once a challenger becomes an incumbent, he or she becomes part of the very machinery that creates discontent. After two or three terms the once successful fresh face can no longer carry the mantle of the crusader and must rely on the same name recognition, personal contacts, and fund-raising ability for the slick media campaign that incumbency provides and on which all incumbents rely.

All of this discussion is generalization, and generalization never applies accurately to all cases. In many state legislative districts it is possible for a legislator to know almost every voter personally; in those cases no amount of money can beat a well-regarded incumbent. Some legislators — particularly at the state level — have enough money of their own to turn down all offers of campaign help in order to preserve their independence. Such happy circumstances, when they occur, however, are exceptions to the standard pattern. Even when incumbents appear so strong that they are never, in fact, challenged, their strength is predicated on their ability to raise money. Having lobbyist friends with money, then, is to a politician what fire insurance is to a homeowner.

It may appear to the reader that I am more cynical about this process than is warranted. However, my conclusions about the power of money have nothing whatsoever to do with a low esteem for human nature. Rather, it is the intentionally conservative design of all legislatures that inevitably leads legislators to rely on the things that money will buy for reelection rather than on other things that money won't buy — such as passionate voter support. Most of what people with money (and that usually means business) want from a legislature is that it do nothing, and "nothing" is exactly what a legislature is consciously, deliberately, and purposefully designed to do. Inevitably, then, legislators gravitate toward a business constituency for whom they can actually deliver, rather than toward other constituencies for whom they cannot deliver.

We now come to a legislature's structural inertia and how that works for business. Because of the design of a legislature, a senator, representative, or state legislator quickly learns that he or she cannot develop passionate, committed independent voter support as a reward for positive accomplishments. The very structure of a legislature absolutely guarantees that during his or her career a legislator will have few positive accomplishments no matter how hard or selflessly he or she works. Therefore, *faute de mieux,* most legislators do the next best thing politically, which is to cultivate the support of those who have money and want help preventing other legislators from doing anything. The irony of all of this, however, is that for very good reasons it is almost impossible to change the structure of a legislature without providing a cure that is worse than the disease.

All legislatures have consciously, deliberately, and purposefully created a process that allows very bad legislation to be killed silently and efficiently without anyone's being personally responsible for the legislation's demise. That is exactly how we handled the plumber's licensing bill for years in West Virginia. I have seen instances where a particular piece of pernicious legislation with strong, organized support was quietly killed in spite of the fact that every legislator in the process alleged that he or she supported the bill. Given that almost all bills that are introduced into any legislature are attempts by one group to steal money or other advantages from another group (usually in the name of economic development or social justice), the genius of a legislature is that every individual member can be yelling "yes! yes!" at the top of his or her voice, while the process as a whole can be whispering "no! no!" softly but effectively.

At the heart of legislative inertia is the bicameral structure of almost all legislatures. This particular design is so essential to the smooth operation of a branch of government that is deliberately designed to be conservative that had we not inherited such a system from the priests, barons, and knights of yesteryear we would have invented it. In fact, after World War II when Norway's government was redesigned, Norway adopted a parliamentary system with one house. Within a few years, however, Norway's single-house parliament divided itself into two houses and proceeded to do business as if it had originally been set up with a senate and lower house.

The reason for bicameralism in general and for Norway's self-imposed reorganization in particular goes to the internal power structure of any legislative body. A legislature attracts all types of people: Some are smart, while others are stupid; some are experienced, while others have had no prior acquaintance with government; some are honest, while others are corrupt; and some have common sense, while others have none. The result of this mixture is that any legislature requires an internal leadership structure that can organize a body of anywhere from thirty to 500 members. When I was a member of the lower house of a state legislature, I found that most of the power in that body, which consisted of 100 members, was wielded by about nine persons. The speaker of the house, the chairs of the finance, judiciary, and education committees, the majority and minority leaders, and the three minority members of the rules committee pretty well decided what the house's agenda would be. The rest of us were nothing but high-class, elected lobbyists soliciting favorable action from that power structure. It was the speaker and his close associates who determined committee assignments, the allocation of office space and staff support, and appropriations for general junketing.

Control of a member's committee assignments, staff support,

and travel budget brings with it a certain control of a member's vot-
ing record. Control of the agenda alone allows the leadership of any
house to make extortionately unequal trades with members, such
as appropriations for a member's local health department in return
for the member's vote on wholesale tax revision. Furthermore, leadership positions in legislatures are not allocated on the basis of ideology but rather on the basis of personal relationships. Frequently
it is possible to have a presiding officer of a house who has an ideology somewhat at odds with a majority of that house's members,
since the presiding officer is elected by a majority vote of the majority party. Thus, in a 100-person house, if there are fifty-one Democrats to forty-nine Republicans, twenty-six Democrats can elect the
entire leadership of the house.

The danger of unicameralism, therefore, is that a minority representing one interest group can gain control of the whole shooting-
match and run its own agenda for several years. The solution to this
problem has always been the second house of a bicameral legislature where the leadership is entirely different from the leadership
of the first house. Although within each house of a bicameral system it is possible for legislators to trade with one another for their
own account — staff, travel, office space, and even help-your-
friends bills — it is far more difficult to make such trades between
houses. The trades between houses all relate to the business of government — namely, bills passed in exchange for other bills passed,
amendments accepted in return for other amendments rejected, and
bills killed in exchange for other bills killed.[5]

A bicameral design may prevent the elected leadership of one
house from running off with the family jewels, but even more cumbersome machinery is needed to create a truly conservative institu-

---

[5]In this latter regard "killing" a bill is very different from "defeating" a
bill. When a bill is "killed," it dies a silent death without any embarrassing
recorded vote that might haunt a responsible member on election day.
When a bill is defeated, everyone is on record, often an unenviable position for conscientious members who must vote against constituents' pet
projects.

tion. Consequently, within each house there is a complicated committee system that is designed to protect the family jewels from interest groups within that single house, while at the same time allowing legislators to keep their jobs. Through the use of the committee system the leadership can assure the quiet demise of most rapacious bills, even when interest groups with both money and direct, election-day organization are pressing for passage. For example, the presiding officer can usually determine to which committee a bill will be referred. Some committees meet frequently and are staffed by the better class of legislators (state judiciary committees, for example), while other committees meet infrequently and are staffed by the house's lowbrows (state public institutions committees, for example). Furthermore, certain committees are favorably disposed to particular types of legislation, while other committees are unfavorably disposed. It makes a great deal of difference, therefore, to which committee a bill is referred.

The agendas of both Congress and the state legislatures are very crowded. Although both Congress and the legislatures of the big states like New York and California meet all the time, in the smaller states legislatures typically meet sixty or ninety days a year. Even the Maryland legislature meets only ninety days a year. In general, the committee chairmen control the agendas of their respective committees, and unless a particular piece of legislation has overwhelming support of a real rather than feigned variety, it is likely to find itself on that part of the agenda that the committee never gets around to. From the point of view of legislator job security, crowded agendas and control of the agendas by committee chairmen make it possible for legislators to support almost everything that their constituents want in perfect confidence that nothing will ever pass. I have seen legislators send letters with impassioned pleas to committee chairmen to move particular bills, although the same legislators in the halls or in the evening at a local bar tell the same chairmen to kill the same bills.

The preceding brief discussion is not intended as an exhaustive description of how every legislature works, but it should be obvious from just this cursory glance that killing a piece of legislation is about a hundred times easier than getting a piece of legislation passed. Furthermore, whenever business wants to commit billocide, it is not necessary to lobby the entire membership of both houses. It is sufficient if only one house rejects the bill, and in order to achieve that desirable goal, it is not even necessary to lobby the entire membership of even one house. Ownership of either a presiding officer or the committee chairman to whose committee the bill is referred will usually consign the issue to the bottom of the agenda, but failing that, all one needs is a majority of the members of a committee or even a subcommittee. When the leadership in general and a committee chairman in particular are hostile, a few strong, militant troops strategically placed among the membership as a whole can usually work wonders by the use of obstructive parliamentary tactics such as the threat of a filibuster.

In the legislative process it is not necessary for business to have the vote of any particular legislator on every business issue; it is only necessary that business have a legislator's vote on all the business issues that do not directly affect the insular interests of that legislator's constituents. Thus a legislator from a rural county can be adamantly against business when the question is whether to build a hydroelectric dam in his county that will flood numerous square miles of his constituents' farm land, while at the same time the same legislator can be for business on all environmental issues because his constituents live in a pollution-free area anyway.

A legislator concerned more with his or her own reelection than with the public interest (whatever that is) will find it financially rewarding to be pro-business in all instances where the interests of business represent no conflict with his or her own constituents' interests. Indeed, many representatives and senators who come from states that have never produced a drop of oil are passionately committed to the oil depletion allowance of the Internal Revenue Code, and in return, they are handsomely supported by oil lobbyists at election time. For reasons consistent with this pattern, West Virginia representatives and senators regularly receive heavy campaign contributions from maritime interests although West Virginia has no seaports!

Of course none of this is to say that it is impossible to get *any* legislation passed at either the state or national level. Legislation, for good or ill, passes all the time; the point, however, is that a lot less of it passes than most people ever imagine. Passing legislation requires a level of organization and financial support that few interest groups possess. In 1981 the Reagan administration accomplished a major restructuring of both our tax system and the national government in spite of all the forces favoring inertia and strong opposition from the social welfare constituencies. The recent Reagan revolution, in fact, is an example of a rather standard pattern; revolutionary legislation is not lobbied through by private interest groups at all but, rather, like the Reagan changes, is lobbied through by the executive branch. Furthermore, some historical periods are more auspicious for legislative change than others. The period from 1972 to 1978, for example, brought a high level of citizen activism and legislative idealism. The Vietnam war, the discontent of the under-30 generation that perceived unfulfilled promises of social justice, and the social strains caused by integration and the rural/urban migration of the 1960s brought us six years of extensive legislative activity. Even then, however, better than 95 percent of all the bills introduced in most U.S. legislative assemblies never passed.

Ordinary legislators who lack personal fortunes and who refuse to play the money game end up returning to private life. Business, then, ends up with a lock on the legislature because the only source of big bucks that most politicians have is the coffers of business. Furthermore, judges understand this entire phenomenon. On my own court, for example, one judge is a former state senate president, another judge served many years as a legislative staff member, and I am a former member of the house of delegates. That's three out of five! Throughout the federal judiciary the courts are staffed by former state legislators, former party executive committee chairmen, and even former congressmen and governors. In general judges do not rail against the inherent venality of the legislative process because they understand perfectly well that the cures may be worse than the disease. But at the same time, they understand the process well enough not to be overwhelmed by theoretical arguments emerging from the eighth-grade civics texts that enjoin all lawmaking to be conducted in the legislatures.

The strange thing, however, is that not only do the judges understand the ironies of the legislative process, but legislators understand them perfectly well themselves. This returns us to the point I made in chapter 3 that legislators as individuals and legislatures as collective entities have almost given up on being the supreme lawmaking branch. There appears to be a failure of will on the part of the legislative branch to tinker at our present system, to return more decision making to the legislatures, or, put another way, to arrest the further transfer to the courts of what used to be legislative lawmaking authority.

In this regard it is valuable to explore just one of the counterproductive changes that the Congress has made recently in its own organization.[6] In the days before 1974, when the seniority system was in place, there was a comparatively efficient hierarchical power structure in Congress. All the rewards in terms of delivering some benefit or other to one's own constituency lay in supporting the leadership and biding one's time until the Grim Reaper pushed one up the seniority ladder. The internal congressional reforms of the 1970s, however, that destroyed the seniority system had the additional, unintended effect of placing most tangible political rewards for congressional service on the side of mavericks and self-promoters. The advent of televised congressional proceedings, the increase in accredited journalists from 1,649 in 1964 to 3,748 in 1984,

---

[6]Here I am borrowing again from the work of Gregg Easterbrook, at note 3 above.

and the opportunities presented by the national media for show-boating all created incentives for legislators to become, in the words of Senator Robert C. Byrd, showhorses instead of workhorses.

In 1964 there were but forty-seven meaningful chairmanships in both houses of Congress combined. By 1984, however, the show-boating instincts of the members had produced 326 separate chairmanships, and even allowing for those who hold more than two chair positions, 202 of 535 representatives and senators — 38 percent — are now chairmen. Furthermore, although top staff jobs in Congress pay from $46,000 to $56,000 a year, the average staff salary is $25,000, which means a staff turnover rate of roughly 40 percent a year. Although young and inexperienced staff come to government with new ideas and full of enthusiasm, they lack an institutional memory and are largely ignorant of the real-life problems of states, businesses, unions, and other entities that they have been hired to regulate. Representatives and senators, in turn, have little time to attend to the actual work of governing. A typical senator will receive 3,000 pieces of mail a day; in 1983, as a result of expanded air service and cheaper fares, 5 million individuals visited the Capitol grounds, and a substantial number of them "visited" their representatives and senators. Representatives and senators who, thirty years ago, could drive to Washington for the session and remain there because of the difficulty of returning regularly to Texas or North Dakota, are now expected to rush home to every state fair and chicken dinner to which they are invited.

The gallery of horribles at the national level, however, is but the story of state legislatures writ large. In 1971 when I first went to our state legislature, I was left in comparative peace because it took five hours to drive from my home county to the state capital. Today it takes slightly over two hours on a beautiful, four-lane highway, and my successors are required to spend fully four times as many hours entertaining constituents as I ever was. The advent of privately recorded, videotaped messages allow even the humblest state legislator to visit his constituents on the local nightly news, and in order to have something to record, he or she too must resort to showboating and the creation of entertaining but seldom important issues.

None of this technology, however, has had an effect on the courts. Judges have no greater incentive to showboat today than they had 200 years ago; judges do not get called or bothered by constituents because they have none; judges are not the prisoners of their mail because, with life tenure or very long elected terms, they can simply throw it away. Judges never have to entertain visitors, nor do they ever have to travel anywhere they don't want to go. In effect, then, while legislators are distracted and diverted more and more from serious work as a result of technology, the courts plod along hardly touched in their way of doing business since the Middle Ages.

All of this is not lost on legislators who have become cynical themselves about the branch of government in which they serve. Although among many legislators, the impulse may not have risen to a conscious level, there is increasingly a feeling of despair about the effectiveness of legislatures on the part of legislators. In fact, many legislators who have commitments to the social welfare constituencies encourage judicial activism as a necessary ingredient to make bland legislation achieve its purpose. I am sure, for example, that many of the key legislators who supported the passage of title VII of the Civil Rights Act hoped that the courts would interpret it more liberally than its plain words necessarily demand. Consequently, instead of legislators' reacting as we would expect to the increasing power of the courts by reorganizing legislative institutions in such a way that most lawmaking authority returns to legislators, exactly the opposite dynamic prevails. The courts, in one sense, have made it possible for legislatures to be irresponsible, and although there is a lot of regret over the situation on the part of many legislators, so far there has been no concerted or effective effort to reverse the process.

Chapter 6

The Administrative Agency: Business' Nemesis

No aspect of the law is potentially as important to a business-person as an intuitive grasp of the relationship of courts to administrative agencies, yet the whole subject of administrative law is among the most confusing and least structured areas in all of jurisprudence. The primary reason for both the confusion and lack of structure is that in administrative law courts are doing the work of politicians and not the work of lawyers. For good reasons, however, courts can't admit that fact.

In essence, courts are needed to supervise administrative agencies because they are subject to little other constituent-oriented, political control. There are roughly 3 million civil service jobs in the federal merit system of which none is elected. In fact, in the entire federal executive branch, there are but two elected officials, and the highest calling of the second is to check, on a daily basis, to make sure that the first is still alive. In state governments there are usually, in addition to the governor, a few statewide elected officials variously called treasurers, comptrollers, auditors, commissioners, attorneys general, or superintendents, all with executive duties. However, even where there are numerous statewide elected officials in a state's executive branch, the majority of a state's civil servants, ranging from 5,000 to hundreds of thousands, depending on the state, are responsible to the governor.

It is practically impossible to fire a civil service employee. The government structure created since 1945 utterly confounds the old government and business axiom that if power is to be exercised responsibly and responsively, it must be somewhat insecure. At the state and municipal levels, particularly in small states and cities, a little employee insecurity may be engendered by threatening to transfer employees or abolish jobs. But in the federal government and the big states, once an employee is in the civil service system only mandatory retirement or cardiac arrest can get him or her out.

Furthermore, the government departments that are theoretically responsible to the president, governors, or mayors are augmented by a plethora of independent boards, agencies, and commissions that are established by Congress, state legislatures, or city councils but are responsible to no one. The Federal Reserve Board, Federal Communications Commission, and state boards of regents (which administer state higher education) are examples of this phenomenon. Typically, these independent boards and agencies have from three to nine members who are appointed by the executive for a term of years with the advice and consent of the legislative branch. Once appointed, however, they become a law unto themselves. In fact, independent boards and agencies are deliberately set up to be entirely free of any political control — not for their own sakes but for the sake of elected politicians who would otherwise be responsible for their decisions.

Clearly the designers of the federal and state executive branches did not create popularly elected, instantaneously responsive, democratic institutions where every employee quakes uncontrollably with terror at the prospect of offending any citizen armed with the franchise. With the advent of civil service, an elected executive cannot even pick his or her own department heads or employees. Presidents and governors may be able to name will-and-pleasure cabinet officers or state commissioners, and each of these may have a few will-and-pleasure deputies, but over 99 percent of the employees in most agencies are civil service. Regardless of how dedicated a political leader is to making significant changes in government, almost all his or her minions will be inherited from previous administrations.

One reason that the courts have been accorded such broad powers to review the decisions of administrative agencies is that court control of executive branch bureaucrats and independent agencies is almost ideal from the point of view of elected politicians. The courts themselves are immune from political control, which not only makes them independent but relieves elected politicians of any responsibility for court decisions. The average elected politician, therefore, watches the interplay between administrative agencies and courts with the same sense of concern with which Churchill watched Germany invade Russia.

The confusing thing for businesspeople, and often also for their lawyers, is that when courts review agency decisions, they infrequently admit in their opinions that they are doing the work of politicians. I once saw a case where a new bank charter had been denied because the owner of a county's largest existing bank was also chairman of a state senate finance committee. The court reviewing the decision to deny the charter perfectly well understood that the banking commissioner was under intense political pressure, but what were the judges to say in their formal opinion? "O.K. guys, we know that the banking commission doesn't want to infuriate Senator Wossname and get its budget slashed next year, but because the new bank charter is justified we'll tell you to issue it and take heat off you." Of course not; a certain tact and decorum is demanded. Judges may know where the bodies are buried, but there is no profit in exhuming them constantly for public inspection. Therefore, in a case of political home cooking like the bank case, the court says that "the banking commission decided the case contrary to the weight of the evidence" or that "the reasons the commissioner articulated for its decision did not comply with the statutory requirements for denying a charter" or finally, if all else fails, that "the hearing mechanism was procedurally defective."

In the bank case the charter got issued without any serious repercussions for the banking commissioner, and the court protected its flanks by obscuring its decision with a smoke-screen of legalese designed to put outraged legislators off the scent. But in cases like this, pages and pages of pseudoscholarship that manipulates legal doctrine exclusively to reach a preconceived result will not give a businessperson much guidance about what a court is likely to do in future bank cases when a charter is denied for legitimate rather than political reasons.

Unfortunately, however, even if we set aside for a moment considerations of tact and diplomacy, there are other, compelling reasons why courts cannot forthrightly admit that they are political supervisors of administrative agencies. Courts simply don't have the staff to review every two-bit bureaucratic decision, and if they ever admitted that they review substantive decisions (as opposed to reviewing whether the administrators have followed the law or proper procedure), they would be flooded with more appeals than they could handle. The felicitous smoke screen of what is called "administrative law" serves the purpose of keeping appeals to the courts within manageable numerical limits.

Some administrative law, of course, is just exactly what it appears to be. Administrative agencies frequently operate like kangaroo courts and enter wholly defective orders or do something that is clearly contrary to a statutory mandate. Although cases that fall neatly into a legal rather than a political profile are fairly common, they are not the cases that are of particular interest or importance to business. It is the political cases that must be understood because they illuminate how the courts have become business' most important ally in its daily struggle with regulators of all stripes.

One of the most important things that court review of administrative decisions does is help compensate for the inherent limitations of immaturity, low level of experience, naive value judgments, and susceptibility to economic or social cooption of agency employees. The itinerant assistants to comfortably middle-age political appointees are often under age 30; they are frequently green in judgment, share a world view based on the current philosophy of the great universities that they attended, and may be insensitive to the diversity of attitudes and interests that exist beyond campus walls. Yet they do crucial staff work.

Many of today's government economists, for example, were once math whizzes in their respective high schools and went off to places like Princeton with visions of Nobel prizes in mathematics dancing in their heads. At the great universities, however, they quickly discovered that to make B-minuses in mathematics they had to work like beavers, and working like beavers was not what they wanted to spend four years doing. But the introductory course in economics saved them from drudgery because they figured out that math jocks can get A's in economics in their sleep. They majored, therefore, in economics and partied for four years until graduation loomed prominently on the horizon. At that point they had to decide whether to go to law school or graduate school in economics. Law school looked boring, and to make matters worse, law students paid full tuition; graduate work in economics, on the other hand, was simply more math jockery, and the graduate school paid the student. Simple decision: Harvard or some other prestigious graduate school in economics.

Four years later a person in this profile has been miraculously transformed from a happy-go-lucky undergraduate into a Ph.D. in economics from a great university. He or she is now every bureaucracy's dream. Yet these men and women never had one moment's interest in the great questions that economics is designed to answer. They never tossed and turned at night wondering: Why are some regions prosperous and others poor? Why is there a cyclical variation in employment? How much money can a government borrow before it goes bankrupt? How can a government stimulate or encourage industrial expansion and high-wage job creation? Their training largely involved designing mathematical models — an undertaking where the universal operative principle is that the plural of *datum* is *assumptions*! Now, however, they are running a government, and unless someone with a little horse sense looks over their shoulders, their decisions may not bear any relation whatsoever to the real world of chugging steam engines, smelly plants, sweating and indebted workers, or single-industry communities. The policy choices they make may not reflect any understanding whatsoever of Keynes's observation that "in the long run we are all dead."

Perhaps, however, there is one thing worse than B— math students becoming economists, and that is B— economics students becoming lawyers. Some of the greatest drivel in all of legal literature emanates from the word processors of lawyers trained in economics at the undergraduate level who believe that the concepts of marginal revenue, marginal physical product, and long-run average costs (all of which were hot news about 1890) unlock the mysteries of both legal and economic problems. Often, in fact, the articles that economics-trained lawyers write turn from mere drivel into high comedy when the writers begin to "assume" perfect competition, complete knowledge, and no transactional costs. After all, at the simplest level, in a world of perfect competition, complete knowledge, and no transactional costs, we would all be married to the girl or boy of our dreams! The one thing, therefore, that grey-haired judges who have run businesses, represented labor unions, and defended constituents against the onslaughts of government do is make sure that running the real world is based on data rather than assumptions.

In essence, then, when we examine judicial review of administrative agency decisions we see that the courts are being used as a counterweight to certain limitations or imperfections that exist in any bureaucracy. Among these limitations or imperfections are (1) the tendency of agency decisions to be dictated by illegitimate political considerations; (2) immaturity, ignorance, and lack of judgment on the part of agency staff; (3) the tendency of agency decisions to be made with a view to strengthening the power position or funding level of the agency as a whole; (4) employee laziness; and (5) agency lack of flexibility. Often more than one of these imperfections will be prominent in a particular case, but courts seldom address these imperfections directly in their written opinions.

One of the exceptions to this rule, however, is a case decided in 1973 by the U.S. circuit court of appeals for the District of Columbia, styled *International Harvester v. Ruckelshaus*,[1] that involved the question of whether the administrator of the Environmental Protection Administration (EPA) should allow a one-year's suspension of the statutory requirement that all cars be equipped with emission control devices by 1975. Although the case is complicated, it is particularly instructive because it frankly discusses the political function of administrative review.

In 1973 environmental issues were high on the public's political agenda, and a hard, proenvironment position by the Nixon administration's EPA administrator helped make the Republican party acceptable to moderate environmentalists. The mandate of the EPA administrator was comparatively narrow; he was expected to clean up the environment and be an advocate for environmental concerns rather than a judicious balancer of all competing interests. He attracted to his agency personnel who were passionately committed to environmental improvement, and they were, perhaps, even less judicious than he. In the *International Harvester* case the administrator denied suspension of EPA standards for a year, although car manufacturers alleged that it was technically impossible to produce workable emission control equipment by 1975. The federal appeals court, however, reversed the administrator's decision.

Ostensibly the court decision was grounded on the administrator's reliance on technological methodology — in other words, what scientists thought *could* be achieved by 1975 — rather than on actual test results. The court found that the administrator had inappropriately evaluated whether the risk of erroneous denial of suspension outweighed the risk of erroneous grant of suspension. The court's opinion was written by Judge Harold Leventhal who was candid enough to admit that in such an important case the function of judicial review is to transfer a major national policy decision from an administrative agency that is under heavy political pressure to fulfill a narrow mandate to a less political and more broad-visioned federal court. In Judge Leventhal's own words on this subject,

---

[1]478 F.2d 615 D.C. Cir. (1973).

> It was the judgment of Congress that this court, isolated as it is
> from political pressures, and able to partake of calm and judi-
> cious reflection would be a more suitable forum for review than
> even the Congress.

Judge Leventhal made it clear that it was the responsibility of
the court to consider the interests of every constituency that might
be affected by the decision and not just the legitimate governmental
interest in cleaning up the environment. In this regard the opening
passage of the court's opinion pointed out:

> The automobile is an essential pillar of the American economy.
> Some 28 percent of the non-farm workforce draws its livelihood
> from the automobile industry and its products.

The EPA administrator, of course, had acted perfectly properly.
He had been given a mandate by Congress to eliminate automobile
pollution, and he bravely took on the United States' most powerful
industry. By being inflexible and unaccommodating to the industry,
the administrator kept constant pressure on the manufacturers, yet
in the background there lurked the broader question of what would
happen to the U.S. economy if the manufacturers were not crying
wolf about their capacity to meet the statutory deadlines on emission control. When one out of seven jobs depends on automobiles,
the conservative play is to assume that the manufacturers are not
crying wolf, and in *International Harvester* the federal court made the
conservative play. In reversing the administrator the court deflected
the adverse political repercussions that a year's suspension might
have entailed for the president, and at the same time allowed the
EPA administrator to continue to be a zealous advocate for environmental improvement.

For every case like *International Harvester*, however, that reflects
the problems of court supervision of agency political decisions at
the most exalted level, there are countless thousands of cases that

involve nothing but agency laziness or gross screw-up. A commonly heard expression among government employees is "It's good enough for government work," and a substantial number of them mean it. When business has a problem with government, business must often penetrate layers of administrative personnel to find some responsible, conscientious employee who can make things move. Business is constantly at the mercy of semiliterate government functionaries who resemble in grace, charm, and dedication those most prominent of all government clerks, U.S. postal employees. Only Federal Express or Emery can save us from the post office, but when millions of dollars and thousands of jobs are involved, judges can usually make lazy, stupid, or reluctant bureaucrats do what the law says they are supposed to do.

A recent case in the West Virginia supreme court exemplifies how courts help business combat agency laziness or incompetence. A few years ago the West Virginia legislature gave the state health department authority to pass on new hospital construction and hospitals' purchases of expensive equipment. New state regulatory schemes for hospitals have sprung up everywhere because federal statutes have made such cost containment legislation near-mandatory. Before a hospital may buy a multimillion dollar, diagnostic machine, it must obtain a "certificate of need" from the appropriate state agency, usually the health department. In West Virginia the statute granting this power to the health department establishes time periods during which the department is required to rule on hospital applications. If, for example, a hospital's application is incomplete, the department must, within fifteen days, inform the applicant and also specifically point out what information must be supplied to complete the application.

In 1984 a Clarksburg, West Virginia, hospital applied to the health department for permission to buy an expensive diagnostic machine but received no action whatsoever on its application. When the hospital inquired about the delay, the department informed it that action on all applications had been "suspended" pending the drafting of the department's rules and regulations pursuant to an internal department policy. Instead of sitting down to a thirteen-hour day and turning out a comprehensive set of regulations in quick order, the department just worked its leisurely eight-hour day staggered with lunch and coffee breaks. The department's response to the urgent petitions of its constituents was simply, "Wait until we get good and ready to talk with you!" The hospital knew that an alternative to such abuse was available in the state supreme court where it got a writ of mandamus that required the department to act forthwith on its application.

The administration of health cost containment legislation presents endless opportunities to examine permutations and combinations of the five problems inherent in administrative agencies I listed above. The New Jersey supreme court confronted a perfect example of administrative agency lack of flexibility in a case called *Irvington General Hospital v. Department of Health of the State of New Jersey*.[2] The problem in the *Irvington* case was that to prevent the high costs associated with the duplication of expensive hospital facilities, the New Jersey Department of Health had written regulations that prohibited the construction of new hospital beds in an area where an existing hospital had available beds. Yet the court reversed the health department's denial of a certificate of need to Irvington in spite of the fact that Irvington could not show a shortage of available beds.

In reversing, the court pointed out that, although the health department may have acted perfectly properly under the published guidelines, aged patients need to be close to relatives; the available hospital beds to which the department referred as grounds for denying Irvington's application were all in crime-infested areas where visiting relatives were likely to get mugged, while Irvington was in a safe neighborhood; and (if we read a bit between the lines) Irvington was a good hospital while the other hospitals in the vicinity weren't worth a tinker's damn. The *Irvington* case simply stood for this: Bureaucrats are understandably reluctant to twist and bend regulations to consider such politically unpopular and explosive facts as Hospital X is competent while Hospital Y is a death trap.

---

[2]374 A.2d 49, 149 N.J. Super. 461 (1977).

Judges, on the other hand, have the security to point out the obvious, or if they are of a mind, to take the obvious into consideration while crafting their orders in tactfully less offensive language. Rigid mathematical formulas regulating hospitals, when carried to their logical conclusions, imply that a vacant bed in a bad hospital must be filled before a new bed in a good hospital may be constructed. Both patients and judges, however, think that's stupid, and so would legislators if they got into the details of regulation enough to think about it.

Today both hospitals and doctors are flocking to the courts to appeal cost containment decisions because the courts are more flexible than the health departments. Certainly, in light of the salaries paid by state government, there is a high likelihood that health department bureaucracies will be staffed by mechanical-minded technicians. But in the area of flexibility, the difference between courts and administrative agencies is not entirely attributable to differences in salaries, job security, or even political experience. Because administrative agencies deal with a far greater volume of work than any court, it is almost essential that an agency promulgate broad rules and try to fit every issue that comes before that agency within those rules.

These observations lead us to some ironic conclusions about government and the indispensable role of the courts in the administrative process. In the dispatch of the government's everyday business, flexibility, case-by-case exceptions, and special rules are not particularly desirable because discretion is likely to be abused for political purposes rather than applied objectively and evenhandedly. In the *Irvington Hospital* case, for example, it is difficult to imagine how the agency could have created appropriately flexible rules without so eroding necessary general standards as to make all standards entirely subjective. Administrative agencies, therefore, not only lack the proper institutional structure in terms of quality of personnel, job security, and political experience to permit the informed use of extensive discretion, but extensive discretion is a positive disadvantage in dispatching most of the government's business because of the potential for political abuse.

Courts, however, are used to the exercise of wide discretion. Law is superficially an exercise in the application of broad general rules. Yet as was pointed out in chapter 2, there are so many rules in the court-made, decisional law that law is really an exercise in rule selection. In almost all complicated lawsuits, the real question is not how to apply the legal rule to the facts of the case, but rather which legal rule to select as applicable to the case in the first place. When we look at the strange process by which courts substitute their judgment for the judgment of administrators, it is important to remember that the branch of court-made jurisprudence called "equity" is devoted, in large part, to rule bending and exceptions to rules.

Although there are thousands of statements in reported cases of what equity, as a field of jurisprudence, is supposed to be, I think that the best definition is still Aristotle's:

> When the law speaks universally . . . and a case arises . . . which is not covered by the universal statement, then it is right, where the legislator fails us and has erred by oversimplicity, to correct the omission [and] say what the legislator himself would have said had he been present and would have [wanted to] put into his law had he known [the particular circumstances of its enforcement]. . . . This is the nature of the equitable, a correction of law where it is defective owing to its universality. [*Ethics*]

In areas outside of administrative law, judges apply equitable principles without appearing to do violence to either the predictability or universality of the law.

Equitable exceptions abound even in areas apparently governed by iron-clad statutes. For example, both the statute of frauds and the Uniform Commercial Code require certain types of contracts to be in writing, but because people often don't know that certain agreements must be written or they rely on oral contracts when they assume good faith on the part of the other party, courts have crafted equitable exceptions to the requirement that contracts be in writing.

Consequently, courts have both the conceptual tools and the experience to make the administrative process more flexible, while at the same time keeping equitable or discretionary powers out of the hands of politicians who would inevitably be tempted to self-deal.

The *International Harvester* case is an example of courts' changing the nature of the decision maker and in so doing changing the considerations that inform the decision. The West Virginia hospital case is an example of courts' forcing administrators to act, and the *Irvington Hospital* case is an example of courts' applying flexibility to administrative decisions. The case of the bank charter denial is an example of how administrative discretion may be an open invitation to venal self-dealing. But there is yet a more prominent but less obvious type of agency self-dealing than the venality we encountered in the bank case. Elected politicians self-deal by trading decisions for campaign contributions, speaking fees, outside employment, or jobs for friends. In the bureaucracy, however, the most pernicious self-dealing takes an entirely impersonal form: It involves trading government decisions for the health of the agency's bureaucracy as a whole.

It should hardly come as a surprise to businesspeople (particularly in large corporations) that the function that all bulky bureaucracies maximize is upward mobility for the bureaucracy's middle-level management. Among other things, that's what business mergers and acquisitions are all about. One of the primary ways that government bureaucracies augment their budgets and staffs is to expand the areas over which they have regulatory control. Typically regulatory statutes accord the agency itself power to promulgate rules and regulations that will further some broad regulatory purpose. The difficulty with this scheme, which the eighth-grade civics model never contemplates, is that regulation *per se* is a desirable goal for any agency.

When bureaucratic empire building prompts the creation of new management positions the effect on business can be disastrous. Bureaucracies abhor vacuums, and, inevitably, any idleness will be replaced by activity. When governmental agency personnel have nothing to do, they undertake "research" into their general area of responsibility and ask questions that others, usually business, must answer. In this process, however, business must then underwrite the cost of preparing answers to government's questions. Although the courts are not able to eliminate these problems altogether, when properly petitioned they can keep them within manageable limits.

This chapter's discussion of administrative agencies returns us, finally, to the major thesis of this book — namely, that business has political problems in the courts as well as legal problems. Notwithstanding that courts write opinions that manipulate legal doctrines when they reverse or sustain agency decisions, the factors that dictate court rulings are often never touched on in court opinions.

Therefore, when a hospital wants to challenge denial of a certificate of need by a state health department, it must remember that it is presenting a political issue as well as a legal issue. If the hospital couches its arguments in exclusively legal terms — such as, What did the legislature intend? Did the agency allow a complete hearing before drafting its rules? Is the agency decision contrary to the weight of the evidence? — then the hospital misses its greatest opportunity to prevail. Somehow the hospital's counsel must impress on the court the realities of health care. A hospital that is on the receiving end of some rigid mathematical formula must emphasize the human side of its problem and show that some hospitals are death traps; that patients want to be in hospitals in crime-free neighborhoods where relatives can safely visit; and that doctors may not recommend tests that cannot be done in their own hospitals because they don't want to lose business. When we talk about how doctors behave, courts are more likely than administrators to recognize an understandable, if not commendable, human failing and figure out a way around it rather than demanding a head-on, no-win confrontation with human nature.

Political arguments, however, are not necessarily arguments that many lawyers are trained to make or even comfortable in making. Furthermore, they may not be arguments that can be made entirely in the context of the formal judicial process. Only limited information can be conveyed in the course of a half-hour appellate argument. Even the written briefs (which usually have no space limitation for appendixes) cannot present enough of the extensive background information about the nature of a given industry — health care, for example — that judges ought to understand before making their decisions. The persuasiveness of briefs, no matter how interestingly written, is limited by the natural inclination of judges to play with their grandchildren or go to cocktail parties rather than read volumes of material. Yet as the regulation of business expands on a yearly basis, the courts will increasingly become the final arbiters of regulatory policy, and business must devise better ways of educating members of the judiciary.

Currently most of business' lobbying resources are expended on legislatures and executives. In my own estimation, this means that about 90 percent of business' informational resources are spent on only 50 percent of business' political problems. As the lack of consensus and the cumbersome structure of the legislative branch that I discussed in chapter 5 continue to demand passage of vague statutes designed to accomplish loosely defined purposes, more and more of the United States' regulatory policy choices will fall into the hands of judges through the process of administrative review. That simple fact alone means that some reallocation of informational resources is called for, but the great obstacle to such reallocation is the stubborn and principled resistance of courts to succumb to traditional lobbying tactics. As we shall see in the next chapter, however, lobbying can take many forms, one of which is education.

Chapter 7

Feeding Information
to Judges

Courts are important both for the cases that they decide and for the cases that they *do not decide*. Roughly 94 percent of all lawsuits filed are settled before trial, and many potential suits are settled after lawyers have been contacted but before papers have been filed in court. Courts decide individual cases, but in so doing they create a body of rules that guide the voluntary ordering of business' most important affairs. The litigation process casts a shadow of court-created, settlement-guiding rules, and most business transactions involve bargaining in that shadow.

Ironically, the trial courts, which have the greatest access to information, have the smallest impact on determining what the law's shadow will look like, and the appellate courts, which have the least access to information, have the greatest impact. As was discussed in chapter 2, the workhorse of the judicial system is the single-judge trial court where the litigants, lawyers, and witnesses have a lengthy, face-to-face encounter with the judge. At the trial court level the parties can present prodigious quantities of information, but more important, because the judge must sit on the bench and preside while witnesses are called and exhibits introduced, a trial court judge is an *involuntary* consumer of information. In trial courts there are also informal occasions such as pretrial

135

conferences, in-chambers discussions, and settlement conferences, where information flows through the give-and-take of relaxed conversation.

In the trial court the focus is on what happened in a given case and not on what the legal rules governing that case should be; it is assumed that the rules that will govern the case have already been established elsewhere — either in the legislature or in the appellate courts. But what is of concern to business in the long-run is not the resolution of any particular case but the law generated in specific suits that will govern business in a general way *out of court*. For example, if business loses an "unfair firing" case in the highest court of a state and the opinion changes employment law, business will not litigate employment cases. Rather, business will change its personnel policies and accept whatever inefficiencies result, which is an exercise in anticipatory voluntary settlement.

Appellate courts shape the contours of the law, but in appellate courts, as opposed to trial courts, workload, procedural rules, and organizational structure restrict the flow of information, and high court judges consequently operate in splendid isolation. Appellate courts, like all courts, are busy. Oral argument in any case, no matter how important, is limited to between forty minutes and an hour for both sides combined. Typically, appellate rules will allow each litigant thirty minutes to present its side of the case. Many appellate courts allow oral argument only when *the court* believes such argument will be helpful, and even when an appellate court permits oral argument, the court frequently terminates arguments before the expiration of the formal time allowed. The result of this information gathering system is that appellate judges are only *voluntary* consumers of information. An appellate judge's information comes in the form of the printed record of everything that happened in the trial court below, along with a set of briefs, but the record is not required reading.

A trial judge sits and listens to everything, no matter how stupid or irrelevant. But an appellate judge is part of an organized, collective intelligence. Typically, each appellate judge has two or three law clerks, and in addition there are central staff law clerks, research librarians, clerks of the court, and an administrative staff. To an extent, then, an appellate judge is an administrator; with today's dockets, it could not be otherwise. A typical state intermediate appellate court processes about 500 cases per judge per year. Most of these cases are not complex, and most of them do not present invitations to change the law. Yet all of these cases are of surpassing importance to the litigants involved. And because litigants allot their time and resources according to a case's importance to them, and not its importance to society at large, the amount of time and resources devoted to any one case is not a strict function of the impact that case will have on the contours of the law.[1]

The judges cannot do all of the work that comes before an appellate court; a court's professional and semiprofessional staff must necessarily do much of it. I use the word *semiprofessional* in two senses: Its first and common sense application is to those without legal training, such as professional librarians and skilled secretaries; but its second application is to the recent law school graduates who serve as central staff clerks and judges' personal law clerks. These clerks are "professional" in the sense that they are lawyers who have passed the bar, but they are "semiprofessional" in the sense that they have never practiced law, are very young, and consequently have limited life and political experience. Yet despite their inexperience, these clerks do the bulk of legal research and opinion writing for most appellate courts.

Obviously, if the workload of an appellate court amounts to 500 cases per year per judge, law clerks end up with a great deal of power.[2] A bright and energetic clerk can help a judge sharpen his

---

[1] I can remember one occasion when I was firmly convinced that a man had been unjustly convicted of rape and I devoted substantial personal attention to that defendant's case for an entire term of court — necessarily at the expense of other cases that would have had far greater impact on the civil law that governs business.

[2] Five hundred cases per year per judge is a typical figure, but some courts have much heavier or much lighter workloads. Also many cases included in the 500-case figure border on the frivolous. State prisoners, for example, deluge appellate courts with habeas corpus applications and other proceedings that raise issues that were decided years before. Some appeals are taken simply for the purpose of delay, and other appeals, although of

insights and free him from constant writing to perform other duties. But many law clerks are mediocre, and their slipshod writing and perfunctory research can litter the law for years. *Staffs* of appellate courts and of individual judges differ markedly in their quality. Although the federal courts do not pay their law clerks particularly well ($26,381 a year in 1985), the prestige associated with working for a federal court guarantees a high-quality applicant pool. Whether, however, a judge avails himself or herself of the very best is entirely within the judge's discretion.

At the state level the quality of the applicant pool is spotty at best. States like Massachusetts, New Jersey, and California share with the federal courts sufficient prestige that good graduates come for the experience, but in a state like Virginia the salaries are so low ($21,000 in 1985) that few University of Virginia graduates are attracted to service on Virginia's highest court. Many states are like Virginia in that they pay penurious salaries and also lack enough prestige to attract good clerks for the honor of the thing alone. In West Virginia, on the other hand, we paid $37,165 a year in 1986 for recent graduate law clerks — a salary that allows us to recruit the best from all over the country even though we are not usually regarded as one of the United States' great training grounds for young lawyers.

On the surface appellate courts look like collegial institutions where all decisions are made by majority vote. The court as a whole makes decisions on the ultimate outcome of cases, but the individual judge or clerk assigned to write the formal opinion determines the organization of that opinion and the way the court's result is reached. Often the court does not assign a case to a particular judge; instead, the court assigns the case to a central staff clerk (called a *per curiam* clerk) who, under some scheme of judge supervision, is responsible for preparing the opinion. In some courts the presiding

merit, can be disposed of summarily. It is difficult to compare the workloads of the different courts because the self-reporting method of data collection used by the National Center for State Courts does not impose any standard of measurement. Although the highest court in New York reports it disposed of 684 cases in 1983 and California reports 3,827, one has no idea what types of cases were included or excluded in the samples.

judge assigns the case after oral argument and after the court has taken a tentative vote on a case's outcome. In these courts the judge who receives the case is responsible for giving the facts of the case and the applicable law a careful look to make sure that the court's original, tentative decision was correct. In other appellate courts the presiding judge assigns cases to particular judges or central staff clerks before oral argument. In those courts, the judge or clerk who receives the case is responsible for leading the decision conference discussion and summarizing both the facts of the case and the law that applies to it at the time of decision conference.

To a practicing businessperson the crucial point is that individual judges and their young clerks have a tremendous effect on the decisions that they write. Published court decisions often reflect the opinion of the writer far more than the opinion of the court. But because which decisions an individual judge or clerk will write depends to some extent on the luck of the draw, an individual judge's impact on the law's general rules is somewhat random. In federal circuit courts of appeals there may be as many as twenty-nine sitting judges on one court, but almost all of the cases there are decided by three-judge panels. If a panel is composed of one left-winger, one right-winger, and one moderate judge, the centrist will hold the deciding vote. But random rotation often produces panels of two or three fire-eaters, all with the same ideological prejudices. When this occurs, it's Katy bar the door!

It is possible for a judge to write a so-called majority opinion that states exactly what a unanimous, multimember, appellate court decided to *do* in a case but that also totally misstates the reasons for the decision and thus confuses the law for years to come. In such a circumstance a false shadow is cast, but business will inevitably behave out-of-court exactly as if the shadow were authentic and adjust its operating procedures and investment decisions accordingly.

In 1978 such a situation arose in West Virginia and centered in three separate suits by employees against their employers for work-related injuries. The central issue was the extent to which the state supreme court would uphold legislatively granted immunity to common law suit for employers who subscribed to the workers' compensation insurance fund.[3]

Although three separate cases had been appealed to the state supreme court at the same time from different lower courts, all three cases presented the same legal issue and were consolidated for decisions in one written opinion. The lead case involved a worker by the name of Mandolidis who had been employed in a lumber mill in one of our rural counties.[4] Mandolidis was the operator of a large saw that was equipped with a protective guard over its rotary blade to prevent operator injury. Unfortunately, the protective guard reduced the saw's rate of production, and the employer ordered the removal of the protective guard in order to speed up the saw's output. As a result, Mandolidis cut off several fingers.

So far, Mandolidis had nothing more than a routine industrial accident that workers' compensation would cover. Both employers and employees are careless on a fairly regular basis, and ignoring safety rules is frequently a joint venture.[5] But there was an additional wrinkle to Mandolidis's case because Mandolidis was not a willing conspirator in submitting himself to danger; he was a careful worker who vociferously protested the employer's instructions to remove the guard from his saw. When Mandolidis protested the dangerous working conditions, his employer told him to operate the saw without its guard or be fired, and because Mandolidis needed his job, he reluctantly complied with his employer's direct order.

---

[3]Until recently, workers' compensation was always thought of as a *substitute* for employees' remedies under the general tort law. What employees lose in the amount of awards is offset by the fact that they need not prove any negligence on the part of the employer, and in fact can recover even when the injury is entirely their own fault.

[4]*Mandolidis v. Elkins Industries,* 161 W. Va. 695, 246 S.E.2d. 907 (1978).

[5]Every time I am in the cab of a railroad engine, for example, I observe some highly creative but entirely unauthorized mechanism for overriding the "dead man switch," an apparatus designed to stop the engine in the event that the engineer suffers a heart attack. The reason that engineers override the switch is that it requires them to hold a handle or push down on a foot pedal while the engine is running — something that a healthy engineer finds annoying.

Now the case was no longer a routine industrial accident; rather, it involved a conscious, deliberate, and purposeful decision on the part of the employer to sacrifice the safety of an employee to increased production.

The facts of the *Mandolidis* case were so egregious that the case needn't have been of great moment in redefining the law that governs employer immunity. Our workers' compensation statute denies an employer immunity from common law suit in circumstances where the employer "willfully and intentionally" inflicts injury on the employee. Obviously the court could have decided Mandolidis's case by a simple determination that the employer's actions were of the type that the legislature intended to include under the rubric "willful and intentional." A conservative court might have interpreted the statute narrowly and held that "willful and intentional" applied only to circumstances where the employer deliberately struck an employee or encouraged other employees to engage in a violent altercation. A middle-of-the-road court, however, would have had no difficulty finding that Mandolidis's employer acted intentionally. Placing Mandolidis under the exception to employer immunity, therefore, did not necessarily involve any serious violence to the general scheme; only a rare employer these days behaves like the villain in a Dickens novel. The Court could have written the *Mandolidis* case in four pages, done justice for Mandolidis, and left the workers' compensation scheme in West Virginia undisturbed.

But that is not what happened. The judge who was assigned the case and who wrote the opinion is, by his own admission, a "prolabor," "peoples'" judge who publicly associates himself with the AFL/CIO and the United Mine Workers of America. Furthermore, he is an elected judge who must engage in a contested, statewide, party primary election and then a contested general election campaign every twelve years. It is hardly surprising, then, that he wrote the *Mandolidis* case in such a way as to lead a reasonable reader to believe that employers' immunity from suit for work-related accidents was very close to being abolished in West Virginia by court fiat. It was not the court's simple *holding* in favor of Mandolidis that ultimately caused untold problems for the West Virginia economy, but rather the *tone* of the majority writer's opinion and the way he handled the other two cases consolidated with *Mandolidis.*

The two other cases involved serious industrial accidents. In one case a cascade of slate crushed a mineworker to death. In the other case four bridge workers were injured and another killed when a cable dislodged a work platform and sent the workers plunging into a twenty-five-foot excavation pit. The court should have granted summary judgment for the employers in both these cases because, unlike the *Mandolidis* case, there was no allegation that the employers knowingly and deliberately ordered their employees to work under hazardous conditions. Instead, the state supreme court sent both suits back to the trial court for further factual development, which led to the false impression that the court would never again allow summary judgments in suits for work-related injuries but rather would require such cases to be submitted to juries. This, in turn, led to the spectre of high jury awards in the cases employers lost and horrendous legal fees in the cases employers won. As I indicated in a separate opinion, if either of the two other cases returned after full trial with a judgment for the plaintiff, it would be reversed. But the two other cases never returned to the supreme court; they were probably settled.

The *Mandolidis* case did irreparable harm to the economic health of West Virginia, and, more to the point, it did that harm entirely as the result of gratuitous language that had nothing to do with the court's decision in the case but that altered beyond recognition the law's shadow. Workers' compensation lawyers filed tort suits, then, as a matter of routine whenever there was a serious industrial accident if for no better reason than to avoid charges of malpractice. Employers settled; for many employers, the problem was not as much the threat of big jury awards as it was the legal costs, at $125 a lawyer hour, of defending nuisance suits.

Our court did not get another case squarely presenting a *Mandolidis* issue for six years, and when that case finally arrived, the court gutted the *Mandolidis* opinion. Meanwhile, by 1982 the deterioration of the business climate as a result of the *Mandolidis* decision had reached such crisis proportions because new industry was discouraged from locating in West Virginia[6] that even the AFL/CIO (if, perhaps, not the UMWA, whose members work for captive mines) urged the West Virginia legislature to make statutory changes that all but annulled the original *Mandolidis* decision.

The irony of all this, however, is that only the majority opinion writer and one other judge (defeated in his 1984 bid for reelection) were committed to eroding employer immunity to the extent that the *Mandolidis* case implied. My dissent tried to make that point clear at the time, and although one middle-of-the-road member of the *Mandolidis* court retired in 1980, the Court's 1984 retreat from *Mandolidis* bears out my original conclusion about the opinion's overbreadth. One must ask then, why would any court publish an opinion that went farther in its gratuitous discussion of a terribly important issue than the court intended to go? The answer has to do both with any court's overwork and the internal dynamics of a multimember body.

A court has a certain amount of work that it must dispatch every term; if judges argue and fight over each morsel of language in majority opinions nothing would ever get done. Furthermore, the ultimate weapon in the hands of a judge assigned to write an opinion is to refuse to write the opinion the way his or her colleagues want it written and force them to write it themselves. On the U.S. Supreme Court where every judge has three workaholic law clerks

---

[6]One lawyer of my acquaintance represented a large mining concern in 1979 that wanted to expand its operations into Logan County, West Virginia. The company had spent $160,000 to do core drillings and other preliminary explorations and had found some rich seams of coal. Logan County is one of the most depressed areas of the state, and the company involved planned to invest in an underground mine capable of producing 1 million tons of coal a year. The *Mandolidis* case, however, caused the company to abandon the project because *Mandolidis* created an open-ended liability for coal producers that was both difficult and expensive to insure against. Mining has the most detailed health and safety regulations of any industry; whenever there is an accident, it is almost inevitable that some safety standard has been violated. The money that would have come to West Virginia to open the new mine was invested in Eastern Kentucky instead.

who were editors-in-chief of top U.S. law reviews and where the entire court writes only 141 to 151 opinions per year, threatening to force a colleague to write a case is not too much of a weapon. But on an overworked and understaffed state court, it's hard enough to do one's own work without being forced to do the work of others.[7]

The second reason, however, that cases say things that only the majority writer intends has to do with the internal dynamics of a multimember political body. Different judges have different political agendas, and as in a legislature or corporate boardroom, in order to get along one must go along. Strange as it may sound (because it confounds human nature), judges do not make *explicit* political deals; one judge never says, "I'll vote with you on the *Mandolidis* case if you vote with me on the *Smith* case." The tradition of the legal profession is strong enough that even judges who were once wheeler-dealer politicians believe that explicit case trade-offs are improper, if not downright immoral. But there is a more subtle form of accommodation — perhaps the type of accommodation that one would find in a corporate boardroom — which involves acquiescing at the margin to what colleagues want in return for treatment in kind. A judge, therefore, who is comparatively indifferent to business concerns but who has a crowded agenda in criminal law or civil rights is likely to agree to superfluous and even misleading language in a case like *Mandolidis* in return for free reign to embellish his or her own opinions in similar fashion.[8]

Ironically, in cases that are destined to become landmarks because the contours of the law are uncertain, little if any information is presented during the trial or on appeal about what the contours

---

[7]On the U.S. Supreme Court when justices want to dispose of a case they think is insignificant, they will often write the entire opinion in quotes from older U.S. Supreme Court cases. The purpose of that technique is to avoid hassles over language because it is presumed that if the language has already passed muster in another case it can stand as is.

[8]One of the subjects that is of recurring concern at the Conference of Chief Justices (where the chief justices of the state courts convene twice a year) is the lack of consistency among opinions written by different panels on

of the law ought to look like. "Argument" is different from "information." Most participants in the legal process assume that judges will either follow precedent or think up some new rule based on other received wisdom. But this belief is at odds with how other political leaders make decisions. Legislators and executives import sizable amounts of personal experience into their decisions, but they are also deluged with and force-fed information by outraged constituents, lobbyists, newspaper reporters, and their colleagues. In fact, for all the farce associated with political campaigns, the one valuable function campaigns perform is that they give politicians firsthand information about their constituents. Elected politicians suffer from many disabilities, but isolation from real life is not one of them. Judges do not have, and are not even allowed to have, any of these sources of information.

Politicians, of course, have much more than simple "access" to information. When I was in the state legislature, I used to enter the Daniel Boone Hotel in Charleston through a dark alley, wend my way through the trash cans and piled garbage around the hotel's service entrance, take the servants' elevator to the tenth floor, and then with the utmost stealth, walk up the stairs to my suite to avoid being snagged by interest group spokesmen. As a legislator, to sleep in my own house past 7:00 A.M. required silencing the bell on the telephone (taking the receiver off the hook was too obvious). Furthermore, the volume of incoming *personal* correspondence gave a whole new dimension to the expression "junk mail."

Yet as an elected judge I average only about one constituent telephone call a week, usually from someone who has no idea what courts do, and my incoming mail is limited to throw-away bro-

---

intermediate appellate courts that sit in three-judge panels instead of sitting as a full court. The group dynamics of multimember courts that divide themselves into numerous panels are so byzantine that the politics of the U.S. Supreme Court or an ordinary five-, seven-, or nine-member state supreme court look very straightforward by comparison. Imagine, for example, the group dynamics on the U.S. Court of Appeals for the Ninth Circuit where there are twenty-nine active judges, many of whom have reputations for being militantly ideological but who sit in randomly selected three-judge panels.

chures and reports. Gone are the days when I received a daily pile of personal letters setting forth political positions that required at least a short answer and that in turn required me to think a moment about the problem presented. Unlike a state legislator, representative, or senator, a senior appellate judge need never travel any more broadly than from his or her home to the courtroom! Campaigning at factory gates, meeting chamber of commerce members at their annual dinner, or being deluged with information by constituents at Fourth of July picnics is not part of a judge's job.

As the professional public affairs staff of major corporations are fond of pointing out, lobbying is primarily a matter of providing accurate information. (It is even more a matter of money, as was pointed out in chapter 3, but public affairs staffs are reserved in their candor on that subject.) Everywhere else in politics providing accurate information to the people making political decisions is the way to advance one's cause. Accordingly, it hardly seems heretical to suggest that efforts to do the same with judges are appropriate, at least if we concede that judges act on political and not academic principles.

Management consultants such as Thomas Peters constantly emphasize how important it is for senior business managers to leave the executive suite to talk with salespersons, line employees in the manufacturing process, and customers. Peters calls this "naive listening," but it is actually just an exercise in gathering pure, unfiltered, accurate (and usually unpleasant) information. Judges of high-level courts, unfortunately, do even less naive listening than business executives. Judges are also managers, but when judges make wrong decisions *they* don't lose any money or have to worry about Carl Icahn attempting a hostile takeover. Purists will argue that judges are supposed to get all their information from the briefs and printed records that litigants submit in pending cases so that the adversarial process will purify the data. Politician-lawyers understand, however, that large doses of serious reading are unlikely to be undertaken voluntarily by anyone; therefore, the adversarial system for presenting information to, say, the U.S. Supreme Court, which looks perfect in theory, is woefully inadequate in practice.

Many judges are elevated to the bench exactly because they are proponents of a particular ideology or interest group position. Unless those judges do a lot of growing after they don their black robes (and many do, to the greater glory of the whole system), it is hopeless to appeal to them with "objective" arguments. But it is an unusual court where the majority are not persons who, within the confines of the workload demands, are genuinely inquisitive, open-minded and fair. A convincing presentation of the systemwide effect on employment, investment, business climate, and economic growth of a particular decision will impress these judges. Furthermore, such a presentation instructs a court's understanding of how to write a narrow opinion that does not create a false shadow of what the general law actually is.

At this point *Mandolidis* presents us with another lesson — namely, that the interests of an individual litigant in an important case may be entirely different from the interests of the business community as a whole. In the *Mandolidis* case business in general did not care one fig whether the defendant lumber mill was found liable. What business in general was interested in was simply that the decision in *Mandolidis* not be overbroad. But the employer involved, who was interested *only* in avoiding a damage award, argued the case. In effect, then, the employer defendant in *Mandolidis* did not represent business in general but rather only himself. The result was that the employer attempted to justify his own conduct as "common business practice" and perfectly acceptable — an argument that could have persuaded only the supreme court *chez* Attila the Hun.

If in *Mandolidis* the Court had allowed a well-trained business lawyer to argue the position of *business in general* that lawyer would have dealt with the inadvisability of an overbroad ruling and would have pointed out how such a ruling would encourage frivolous lawsuits, raise costs, and put West Virginia at a competitive disadvantage *vis-à-vis* neighboring states. Furthermore, the lawyer could have *proven* all of these allegations statistically. None of this occurred, however, because the litigation system that has evolved over the last eight hundred years allows little room for the generation of legislative facts. That deficiency might have been of small moment fifty years ago when courts played a less prominent political role; today, however, the problem assumes almost crisis proportions and is at the heart of business's jeopardy in the courts.

As I indicated at the beginning of this chapter, the courts that have the most power have the least information. In this regard, if a litigant were to ask a trial court to change a legal rule, the judge would be compelled to hold extensive *factual* hearings on the matter. If a litigant urged a trial court to narrow employer immunity under workers' compensation, for example, all of the legislative facts that would bear on the problem could be presented, debated, and organized into a coherent pattern.

But trial courts don't make the law; they simply follow precedent, and when all that they are being asked to do is to follow an old rule, there is no need for them to gather facts about the wisdom of the rule. In the *Mandolidis* case the lower court simply dismissed the plaintiff's lawsuit out-of-hand based on old state supreme court cases interpreting the statute on employer immunity. And because in the lower court the employer won, the employer had no incentive to spend money justifying, factually, the wisdom of long-established precedent.

Therefore, when the *Mandolidis* case arrived in the state supreme court there were no legislative facts to support any conclusion whatsoever about the proper scope of employer immunity. But that might not have made any difference because the lawyers could have resorted to a technique known as the "Brandeis brief" (so named after Supreme Court Justice Louis Brandeis who pioneered the technique as a practicing lawyer). A Brandeis brief assembles as many legislative facts as possible from published scholarly papers, statistics provided by government agencies, and commentary from recognized treatises — sources that are generally thought to be neutral. It then supports the legal conclusions it wants the court to adopt with the data collected from outside sources and organized for the occasion. Yet writing such a brief in a concise, convincing manner demands a skill that is not commonly found in ordinary business law firms.

Because the interest of the individual business litigant in any landmark case may be at odds with the interest of business in general, it is as likely as not that the Brandeis brief that the court needs to have before it will have to come as an *amicus curiae* brief — in other words, a brief submitted by an outside group interested in the outcome of the case but not a party to it. After such a brief is produced, however, the real trick is getting judges and law clerks to read it. In my experience, *amicus* briefs have the lowest likelihood of all the papers filed in appellate cases of being read by the judges. *Amicus* briefs are usually of low quality and simply repeat the same technical arguments that the parties to the suit have made themselves, although theoretically, *amicus* briefs should be the most informative of all the arguments submitted on the societywide effects of the different positions a court might take in a potentially precedent-shattering case.

Of all U.S. industries, the media have the most at stake in the courts. Unsurprisingly, the media are smart enough to lobby judges outside the adversarial process. Newspapers, television, and radio are at the mercy of courts because only the courts, through interpretations of the first amendment, can protect them from the wrath of everyone else. Some of the most elaborate decisional law in the United States centers in protection of the media from libel and slander actions. The protective rules to guarantee "robust free discussion" under the first amendment grant the media a unique insulation from legal recourse. Not only does the media's preferred legal position make it nigh impossible to collect a judgment against media defendants, but also the special summary judgment rules the courts have crafted in libel cases make it easy for the media to escape burdensome legal fees. The media, of course, lobby for their own positions *in the media* and not just through briefs filed in appellate courts!

The Gannett Corporation, a large media conglomerate that

owns newspapers across the country, as well as *USA Today*, has even gone one step further and inaugurated a program of one-on-one lobbying of appellate judges. In December 1976 the Gannett Corporation invited me to attend a "media and the law" seminar at The Greenbrier Hotel in White Sulphur Springs, West Virginia. The seminar's director was Professor Fred Friendly of the Columbia University School of Journalism, and the moderator for the working session was Professor Arthur Miller of the Harvard Law School. It was a three-day luxurious vacation with Gannett and the Ford Foundation bearing the expenses in equal shares. Out of approximately sixty participants, fifteen were judges, but the representation heavily favored appellate judges from the Fourth Circuit federal appeals court, federal trial court judges, and judges of the highest courts of states. The other participants were reporters, editors, publishers, and miscellaneous academics.

Ostensibly the purpose of the Gannett/Ford Foundation seminar was to discuss reasonable standards for responsible journalism — voluntary guidelines on how the media should handle subjects of concern to the courts, such as sensational criminal trials. But the real agenda of the seminar, if my perception was correct, was to give the media an opportunity to explain its operational problems to judges — legislative facts — in the perfectly reasonable expectation that the judges would keep those problems in mind as they crafted the first amendment law on libel and rights to privacy. Furthermore, by conducting the program at The Greenbrier, the media got what professional lobbyists call "quality time." All lobbyists prefer to explain their cases in the relaxed atmosphere of a lunch or dinner when a public official is undistracted by telephone calls or moving on to another appointment.

How did Gannett and its partner, the Ford Foundation, get away with doing something that would have incited universal outrage if the Tobacco Institute had done the same? The answer lies in both what Gannett is and how the seminar was organized. In U.S. society the media are the good guys, and to the extent that they are not the good guys, there is no one to point that fact out. After all, the media are our only professional bad guy hunters. Furthermore, there is no organized group that perceives itself as an antagonist to the media. Perhaps if politicians were unionized, such a group might materialize, but at the moment most of the people who stand the highest likelihood of being libeled are the public figures who either enjoy or have an urgent need for media exposure. Because there is no group like the American Lung Association to capture headlines over the attendance of powerful judges at a lush spa for a little political indoctrination, Gannett, unlike the Tobacco Institute, had nothing to fear in terms of adverse publicity, and the attending judges, including myself, thought no more of our attendance at the time than if we had been invited to participate in a seminar at the Duke Law School.

Gannett also gave the whole operation the patina of an even-handed, objective academic exercise. The presence of respected academic presenters like Fred Friendly and Arthur Miller, and the inclusion of local law professors and other academics among the participants, gave the appearance that all sides had the opportunity to be heard. That intellectual veneer successfully covered any of Gannett's more humble purposes. Finally, the seminar was successful in terms of almost 100 percent attendance because it was held at the most lavish resort hotel in the United States (although in the winter when rates were low).

Gannett's success is an object lesson in how to present legislative facts to judges in a way that permits them to roll them over in their minds and digest them long before a case emerges that requires their application. But what Gannett can do *directly* the Tobacco Institute and the automobile manufacturers can do only *indirectly*. No judge with an ounce of integrity or the least concern for the appearance of propriety would go off to a spa at the bidding of a private corporation to be propagandized about that corporation's problems in court. Nor would the political world around us long tolerate the laundering of money for such an operation through an apparently objective institute (such as a major university) to achieve the same result. Therefore, to make the whole exercise in presenting legislative facts to judges legitimate and successful, the scheme must roughly parallel the structure of the adversary system and provide a mechanism by which all sides of a controversy can be appropriately represented.

And, exactly as in the adversary system with its arrangement for contingent fees, the people with the deep pockets are required to pay all the freight for *both* sides. I have seen this done very well by the American Enterprise Institute where I once attended a seminar on constitutional law at which the executive director of the American Civil Liberties Union and a notoriously left-leaning law professor from Yale were in attendance. In my experience most lobbyists are content if one allows them *to present* their client's side of any controversy. Again and again public affairs officers emphasize that they are primarily in the business of giving accurate information, so that if asked, they are even willing to provide an objective statement of the other side's case.

This latter point may sound strange, but the success of a lobbyist depends on the degree to which public officials trust him or her. Honesty, in this context, is a money-maker; once a lobbyist misrepresents something or omits an important piece of information, he or she is through. Legislators routinely ask lobbyists for a presentation of both sides because politicians have the same problem judges have: In many political debates only one side has the money to hire paid staff to present the issues in a coherent, manageable form. When I was in the legislature, some of the most accurate information *against* strip mining was provided to me by the lobbyist for Bethlehem Mines who did a far better job of making an environmental case *against* his client than the outraged citizens he was fighting. His position was simply that regulation alone could solve the problems, and he was right.

Judges are not very well paid, and so one of the things that judges and their wives do for recreation is attend judicial conferences and training sessions where the government, a private foundation, or a university pays their expenses.[9] Whenever there is

---

[9] The Greenbrier is a particularly good place for conferences because almost the whole cost of a husband and wife's sojourn there is chargeable to the participant; the difference between a single room and a double room — with two lavish meals a day — is only $20.

funding available to send judges to good schools (such as the program for judges at the University of Virginia Law School that leads
to an advanced law degree after two six-week summer sessions and
a written thesis), there are three applicants for every place. During
the early 1970s when the Law Enforcement Assistance Administration provided money to the state courts to further judges' educations, the American Bar Association's appellate judge section sponsored seminars for appellate judges that were full to overflowing.
Therefore, getting judges into an academic setting for a protracted
period to discuss economics, international trade, labor policy, medical malpractice, or even how the insurance industry works is an
easy task. All university law schools and many foundations such as
the Aspen Institute[10] are more than pleased to sponsor programs for
judges; the problem, however, is always funding. Yet as long as
there is some guarantee of neutrality through participating representatives from all sides, it is perfectly appropriate, and even desirable, for judges to attend seminars and training sessions.

Many of the problems that we encounter in government either
have cures that are worse than the disease or are so firmly part of
an historically inherited system that attempts to change them are
hopeless. Fortunately, the problems arising from the dearth of information available to inform the decisions of high-level courts do
not fall into either category. It is possible to change the way that
policy-making litigation matures for decision simply by raising the
problem of insufficient information to a conscious level and then by
placing that problem within the perimeters of the existing litigation
system. Consequently, business and its lawyers can change the way
appellate courts do business simply by making themselves heard at

---

[10]I once spent six days with the chief justice of the United States at an
Aspen Institute seminar sponsored by the Ford Foundation where the
most important subject discussed was the litigation of job discrimination
cases under title VII of the Civil Rights Act. It is possible, therefore, to get
even the most exalted judges to attend an interesting seminar at a posh
place.

the appropriate time and in the appropriate way when they are before the court.

Most judges sincerely want to be fair, and if at every available
opportunity business asks permission to develop legislative facts
when it looks like a case is about to have precedent-shattering effects, the court system will grant that permission. Yet in thirteen
years as an appellate judge I have never seen a case in our own court
where a business lawyer moved for a remand to the trial court to
allow the development of legislative facts when political issues were
presented or argued on appeal.[11] I have, however, seen such a motion (accompanied by good argument on the part of *amicus* counsel)
in the Supreme Court of the United States.

Admittedly, there is the significant practical flaw in all this that
the landmark, precedent-shattering cases — like *Thor Power Tool*,
discussed in chapter 1 — often sneak up on everyone. But the fact
that the careful presentation of legislative information is not possible in *all* cases of significant precedential import does not mean that
it is not possible in *any* such cases. In this regard the shock troops
in a concerted assault to change the system are the law professors.
As I have indicated before, law professors are to judges what the
New York Times is to politicians — the repository of public opinion.

All states have both bar and judicial associations that meet on
a statewide basis regularly, often in joint sessions. These organiza-
tions are always looking for good programs, and a *free* good program is universally a winner. Academic projects (outside of the
physical or biological sciences) are incredibly cheap, and law professors are eager for grants. Because the problem of inadequate information has long been recognized, law professors will queue up
to do something practical in this area of systemic reform. Although
the whole issue of insufficient legislative information being available
to judges is not hot news to law professors or political scientists
specializing in the judiciary, it is hot news to most practicing judges.

---

[11]The structure of appellate courts is such that they never hear evidence
themselves. They delegate that function to one-judge trial courts, or in
some cases, to special commissioners of the appellate court appointed by
the court for that purpose.

Judges, it should be remembered, are not intellectuals; they are politicians.

Once the problem of lack of legislative facts has been made a matter of respectable concern and intelligent discussion, it is up to business' lawyers to make a record — either with witnesses or Brandeis briefs — at appropriate stages of the proceedings. In addition business must deal with the problem that companies that cannot afford good lawyers defend many important, precedent-shattering lawsuits. It is useful to intervene at the appellate level with brief-writing help to the party on the business side or to sponsor the preparation of a stellar *amicus* brief, but there is a higher likelihood of success if a case is well handled from the very beginning.

The *Thor Power Tool Co.* case illustrates the problems of developing legislative facts at a late stage. In *Thor Power Tool* both the chamber of commerce of the United States and the National Association of Manufacturers filed *amicus* briefs in support of Thor Power Tool Co. The *amicus* briefs largely repeated the technical legal arguments made by *Thor*: that the *Internal Revenue Code* allows a taxpayer to "write down" the value of unsalable inventory from its cost to its actual realizable value before it has been physically scrapped or sold. However, one can tell from the U.S. Supreme Court opinion (and from reading the actual briefs filed in *Thor*) that neither Thor Power Tool nor *amicus* parties conveyed to the Court how important this procedure was to their operations. The Court analyzed the problem of keeping spare parts around as follows:

> If this is indeed the dilemma that confronts Thor, it is in reality the same choice that every taxpayer who has a paper loss must face. It can realize its loss now and garner its tax benefit, or it can defer realization, and its deduction, hoping for better luck later.[12]

In short, Thor, the National Association of Manufacturers, and the chamber of commerce did little to show that going businesses are

---

[12]*Thor Power Tool Co. v. Commissioner,* 439 U.S. 522, 545 (1978).

different from an orthodontist seeking to write off his capital loss in General Motors stock before he sells the stock. Business had a strong, although not necessarily a winning, argument based on the law, but if business had marshaled a powerful factual phalanx to protect its flank, business might have prevailed.

Furthermore, no one will ever know whether the lawyers arguing for *Thor* were talking to justices or to law clerks. My suspicion is that Supreme Court justices consider tax law both a bore and a chore; it is not a subject that is likely to be high on anyone's political agenda. Judges might understand the difference between physical inventory and stocks and bonds because of their previous life experience; law clerks, on the other hand, would be unlikely to be sensitive to the problem. My bet is that law clerks had almost exclusive control of *Thor*, and it is for that reason that it was necessary to bring the operation of real warehouses to life in the brief.

If a public affairs officer had wanted to convince a supreme court law clerk that the rules governing write-offs of worthless inventory should not be changed, the public affairs officer would have assumed that the clerk understood the Internal Revenue Code and could manipulate it howsoever the clerk wanted. Consequently, the public affairs officer would have concentrated on showing the clerk why worthless inventory is different from other paper losses, and why changing the rule on when a company may write down inventory would have little effect on generating tax revenue, but a major effect on the availability of obscure books or little-used parts. Clerks might have received an argument like that with sympathy, particularly if a convincing link could have been forged between the old tax rules and jobs or economic efficiency.

Both lawyers and judges will resist proposals to enhance the presentation of legislative facts because the proposals will ultimately be understood for what they are — assaults on the language used to articulate court-made policy. Both lawyers and judges have been trained in the language of the law and therefore have an interest in protecting their investment in that particular language. The language of legislative facts is necessarily the language of economics, physics, chemistry, business, accounting, psychology, and sociology. Any regular viewer of C-Span's television coverage of the Congress must have been impressed by the extent to which representatives and senators speak these languages to the exclusion of the language of law.

Obviously, the development of a better and more regularized system for presenting legislative facts to courts is not a panacea for all the ills of business that originate in the courts. Nonetheless, it is highly effective tinkering at the margin of the judicial/political system and is probably enormously cost/benefit effective; it does not necessarily involve *greater* expense in the preparation of a lawsuit, but rather simply the redirection or more effective use of money that is already being spent. Potentially it provides a record with more power and less freight.

Chapter 8

The Bottom Line

The last chapter in any book about social issues is the most difficult to write because we want it to give solutions. But as the Chinese say, the fact that there is a problem does not necessarily imply that there is a solution. In fact, as I have pointed out in the last seven chapters, business' exposure to adverse court rulings is the result of problems elsewhere in government being solved in the courts. Consequently, when there are solutions to problems, those solutions often do nothing more than change the problems.

Reducing business' hazards in court is more like playing a sport than it is like discovering a cure for a disease. Although the pro-business Reagan administration may be able to appoint 250 federal district judges and 75 federal appeals judges by 1988, that simply means that there will be a counterweight to the 206 federal district judges and 56 federal appeals judges appointed by the Carter administration. In real-world politics no one is talking about removing the power of courts to decide issues; the current conservative program seeks only to change the personnel who decide the issues. Therefore, speculating about possible miraculous cures is a waste of time. In the courts, as in competitive sports, the big difference between winners and losers comes at the margin. A ranked amateur tennis player may be distinguished from a good club player by nothing more startling than the effectiveness of his or her second serve.

Therefore, I will recapitulate some practical considerations that should improve business' performance in the courts at the margin. First, courts are often used to get the attention of business or government bureaucracies that will not respond intelligently to legitimate complaints without the cudgel of a court's compulsory process. For example, I once sued Exxon because I was trying to clear title to a cheap piece of real property and Exxon had a magistrate court judgment lien against it for $500. I made no less than five long distance telephone calls to New York, Houston, and Pittsburgh trying to discover to whom I could send a certified check for $500 so I could get a release, only to discover that although Exxon is well enough organized to sue every defaulting credit card customer in magistrate court, it has absolutely no mechanism to collect judgments and release liens!

My simple complaint in court alleged that (1) Exxon had a lien; (2) we were willing to pay the lien; and (3) Exxon would be required to answer our suit by an attorney who could then accept our money and sign a release. Ironically, however, Exxon did not answer the suit; instead its general counsel sent a letter stating that if I would send $250 to him, I could take a default judgment and clear the title. I did exactly that, but the whole exercise was lengthy, expensive, and infuriating for my client, who, if we had wanted to, could have sued Exxon for punitive damages for abuse of process.

Neither my client nor I was particularly interested in getting rich at Exxon's expense; as it turned out, we both had a good laugh and ended up saving $250, which paid the court costs. And that circumstance illustrates an important point: Although many people sue big companies with entirely larcenous intent, many other people have legitimate grievances and are simply looking for some reasonable, good faith dealing. It is a big mistake to assume that every lawsuit originates in a get-rich-quick scheme on the plaintiff's part and must be met with eight-inch guns. Unfortunately, the plethora of lawsuits in which plaintiffs sue for millions of dollars because they have sprained their ankles on snow-covered parking lots leads everyone to assume lawsuits are simply armed robbery by another name. Unfortunately, because defense lawyers automatically trot out the eight-inch guns whenever a summons and complaint arrive, the war necessarily escalates and an expensive dynamic unfolds. The frustrated plaintiff, who runs up against total intransigence after filing suit, must ask for punitive damages, allege pain, suffering, aggravation, humiliation, and anything else he can think of to get the judgment large enough to pay his lawyer.

The leading lawyer representing fired employees in the emerging area of "unlawful discharge" cases is Joseph Posner from Los Angeles. Posner told *American Lawyer* in 1985 that he accepts only 10 percent of the cases he is asked to take and that in deciding whether he will represent a client he asks himself, "Is this something that grabs your gut and twists it, makes you sit up and say, 'Jesus Christ, that's *awful*?'" By his own admission, Posner is looking for cases of long-time employees with good records who are locked out of their offices, humiliated in front of their coworkers, accused of financial impropriety, or just generally hounded out of their jobs.

If Posner is applying the criteria that *American Lawyer* reports, then when he files a complaint the reaction ought to be to send a conciliator rather than a litigator. When the litigation expenses are taken into account, it is cheaper for an employer to buy off the fired employee than to go to court. More important, however, getting the matter out of the legal system prevents the case from becoming unfavorable precedent should the employer lose. What does Sears care, for example, if some local manager flew off the handle at an employee? Company headquarters need not be as emotionally committed to a personality clash as the local manager. This is not to say, of course, that business should settle all cases. Many cases are brought simply for their nuisance value or because, under some Las Vegas parameter, lawyers believe that they might score a big judgment. But lawsuits are settled most cheaply at an early stage, and so too much cynicism about the other side's motives can be expensive.

Next, business must always keep in mind that courts make law in the context of individual cases. This process means that a business must be interested not only in lawsuits to which it is party, but also in all the litigation that is in all the courts, in the same way that it is interested in all the bills that are before Congress or its state legislature. Unfavorable precedent in the law books can be expensive for business because business settles cases in light of precedent that business uses to predict possible in-court outcomes. No single business entity, of course, can take responsibility for all the litigation in a state (let alone the whole country) that might affect it, but business collectively, through its trade associations, can devote a larger share of its political resources to monitoring and influencing court decisions.

In chapter 7, I discussed structural problems in the policy-making appellate courts. At the simplest level appellate courts make their decisions based on the record that emerges from the trial court, and that implies that it is also important for business as a whole to intervene in potentially precedent-shattering cases at the trial court level. If, for example, a small employer is the defendant in an unlawful discharge case in a trial court, other businesses should help the small employer to develop a beautiful, compelling record in the trial court so that if the small employer loses at trial, he or she can appeal with the hope of not only winning but also emerging from the highest state court with a good precedent. Fortunately for business, there are cases that present facts that provide a compelling argument for business's point of view. When a lawyer who wants to litigate a really bad case sues a small business, business as a whole should not lose the opportunity to flesh out the law in a favorable way.

Next, business should remember that in the land of legislatures and administrative agencies, vague statutes, *lex simulata*, and *lex imperfecta* are dangerous. Court power comes in part from courts' ability to pour contents into empty-vase statutes; the more the legislatures fill up the vases, the less the courts have to work with. Overtly pro-business courts are probably a thing of the past; consequently, whatever value vague statutes, *lex simulata,* or *lex imperfecta* had to business in yesteryear, they are likely to backfire today. Robert Nelson, a research attorney and social scientist with the American Bar Foundation, recently reported in the *Stanford Law Review*[1] that the social attitudes of big business' *own* lawyers are substantially more liberal than the social attitudes of the business clients they represent. Out of a large sample, Nelson found that only 37.5 percent of big-firm corporate lawyers gave priority to precedent and continuity in the law, while 43.9 percent chose, as the preeminent legal value, justice in particular cases.[2] This means that even if business could get its own lawyers appointed to the courts for the next twenty years, there would be no substantial change in the way that courts make decisions, even though former business lawyers might view "justice" in individual cases slightly differently from judges from other backgrounds.

Nonetheless, although courts may be on the side of minorities, consumers, and accident victims in ordinary lawsuits, courts are often on the side of business in the administrative agency process. Because courts are the political supervisors of administrative agencies, business should subsidize the development of new theories and creative approaches to administrative agency review. When, for example, agencies demand unreasonable reporting requirements, there is no reason why business should not go to court to get the forms changed or dropped altogether. In West Virginia I have suggested to numerous bar and business audiences during the past eight years that our court would be favorably disposed to listen to such petitions, yet no one has brought such a case. Plaintiffs' lawyers understand that courts will be receptive to new tort theories, but when the bureaucracy whips business, the administrative lawyers react unimaginatively. Perhaps this is because administrative lawyers must do business with the same agencies all the time and

---

[1]"Ideology, Practice, and Professional Autonomy: Social Values and Client Relationships in the Large Law Firm," 37 *Stanford Law Review* 503 (1985).
[2]*Ibid.,* p. 520.

they fear that what they could gain in court they would lose elsewhere through bad will.[3]

Finally, business must make a concerted effort to educate judges. Courts can understand the total circumstances of the average plaintiff in the course of a three-day lawsuit. By contrast, rarely can a court digest all of a business's complex problems in such a short time. Yet these problems have a bearing on the "justice" of any particular case, and so it is important that judges know about them. Business-sponsored workshops, seminars, and degree-granting programs (like the one for judges at the University of Virginia Law School) are all appropriate vehicles for explaining to judges the social consequences that emerge from their individual decisions.

The above summary in mind, I turn to a new subject — the relationship between business and its lawyers. The United States has a tradition of lawyer-bashing, and today even lawyers themselves find self-flagellation such fun that they join the enterprise with irrepressible glee. For example, our last chief justice of the United States regularly accused lawyers of being incompetent, and Derek Bok, president of Harvard University and former law school dean recently observed:

> A nation's values and problems are mirrored in the ways in which it uses its ablest people. In Japan, a country only half our size, 30 percent more engineers graduate each year than in all the United States. But Japan boasts a total of less than 15,000

---

[3]Some of the most abusive agency regulations arise when it costs more to go to court than to comply. My favorite example of an idiotic regulation is the Mine Health and Safety Administration's requirement that end loaders in strip mines be equipped with brake lights. Were this regulation to apply only to newly manufactured vehicles small companies could live with it, but small companies regularly employ used equipment and the installation of brake lights on an old end loader costs about $1,000. How much traffic does MHSA think there is in a strip mine? End loaders are not usually followed around by other vehicles moving at high speed. Yet the only way a regulation like this could be challenged is by a trade association because no one employer could afford the legal fees.

lawyers, while American universities graduate 35,000 every year. It would be hard to claim that these differences have no practical consequences. As the Japanese put it, "Engineers make the pie grow larger; lawyers only decide how to carve it up."[4]

Professor Ronald Gilson has responded to Bok as follows:

> The greater the assurance that the piece of the pie the investor receives will be the same size as he expects, the greater the likelihood that there will be funds for the baker to bake pies. In a world with positive information and transaction costs, developing transactional structures that reduce uncertainty concerning pie division results in more and larger pies. And business lawyers who design these structures create value.[5]

I have no desire to join in the lawyer-bashing game, but it is important for business to recognize that lawyers are as human as executives and that simply because they are members of a learned profession they are not immune to the natural human failings to which we are all prone. Given lawyers' human imperfection, one must ask if the dynamics of business law practice create situations that put the lawyer's and client's interests at odds. If these conflicts can be removed, it may be possible to improve business' performance in the courts at the margin.

Business lawyers do numerous things, many of which are entirely unrelated to the judicial jeopardy that is the subject of this book. First, lawyers advise business how to comply with the law. Everything that companies do is scrutinized by lawyers for such things as potential antitrust violations, environmental compliance, and compliance with the Civil Rights Act. Second, lawyers negotiate deals and prepare papers that allow business to conduct its ordinary affairs with the lowest possible exposure to litigation. Documents like financial prospectuses, long-term leases, and deeds of trust are

---

[4]D. Bok, *Annual Report to the Board of Overseers, Harvard University* (1983).
[5]Gilson, "Value Creation by Business Lawyers: Legal Skills and Asset Pricing," 94 *Yale Law Journal* 239, 312–313 (1984).

the exclusive province of lawyers who are expected to craft their clients' paperwork to give them a decisive edge if a deal goes sour and a lawsuit follows. Third, lawyers litigate for business in the courts.

Increasingly, big business is having the first two categories of legal work — namely, preventive law and paper drafting — done by in-house counsel. In 1983 General Electric's corporate legal staff employed 366 lawyers, which means that if General Electric's legal department were a private law firm it would be the fifth largest in the nation. The high cost of outside legal services has spawned a significant growth in corporate law departments in the last ten years. A 1983 Arthur Young national survey of 183 corporate law departments of varying sizes from all business sectors showed an average growth of 29 percent between 1977 and 1982.[6] As would be expected, small concerns have small in-house legal staffs. However, despite the phenomenal growth of in-house staffs, the one area where both big and small business continue to retain outside counsel is litigation, and in litigation business finds its greatest exposure to judicial jeopardy.

There are three dynamics involving outside counsel that are counterproductive to business' winning the landmark, precedent-shattering cases. The first of these dynamics was touched on in the introduction, which pointed out that business managers are fiduciaries who must be able to justify the fees that they pay outside counsel by reference to some objective standard. Universally, that objective standard is the "hourly charge," which bases fees on the number of hours of lawyer time spent on a client's problem, plus expenses. Dispatching a client's problem through early negotiation, creative settlement offers, and gestures of goodwill is valuable to the client but financially disastrous to the lawyer. Business lawyers

---

[6]Committee on the Corporate Law Departments, Association of the Bar of the City of New York, and Arthur Young & Co., *National Survey of Corporate Law Compensation and Organization Practices* (6th ed. 1983).

regularly engage in a complicated, court-regulated, formal information gathering process (discovery) before beginning serious negotiations with a plaintiff, ostensibly to enlighten themselves about appropriate settlement offers. Occasionally such information is necessary, but most of the time it tells lawyers little that is useful for settlement (although it can be useful in litigation if no settlement is reached). The most important thing that extensive, presettlement discovery does is provide a basis for a healthy fee. Business would be better off if it paid lawyers almost as healthy a fee based on "value of services" and instructed them to settle cases quickly. Part of the reason for this advice is that litigation has costs that are not reflected either in lawyer fees or court judgments. Business must waste valuable time and scarce trained manpower responding to the other side's discovery, preparing for trial, and going to court.

On the other hand, the high cost of business litigation when undertaken by big, classy firms often causes business to settle winnable cases simply because settling is cheaper than litigating. But it is wasteful to use the same high-quality and expensive lawyers for minor matters that business uses for major ones. It is important for business to discourage nuisance suits by fighting frivolous litigation as long and as hard as possible. Plaintiffs' lawyers must pay their own expenses, and a hard line that demands a full trial in every frivolous case will not necessarily be less expensive in terms of the total cost of all suits actually litigated, but it may be cheaper in the long-run because it should discourage lawyers from bringing bad cases. Posner is an example of a plaintiffs' lawyer who engages in a careful "assessment of litigability" before he files suit. If only meritorious lawsuits have a high likelihood of settlement, then plaintiffs' lawyers are encouraged to filter cases out themselves because plaintiffs' lawyers make a lot more money on settlements than they do going to court. Once a lawyer has accepted a bad case he must see it through to full jury trial, which is a lot of work for little return.

There are numerous aspiring young lawyers in small trial firms who would be happy to defend business in the courts for a reasonable fee if they were asked. Outside the big cities, the normal career path for a trial lawyer is to begin by representing plaintiffs and then to move on to representing defendants once he or she has made a reputation. Often business' total exposure in a lawsuit is no more than, say, $50,000. Accordingly, the proper approach is to retain a young lawyer and direct him or her to do as much as possible for $2,000, which basically means walking into court and throwing the case up for a jury to decide. If the case is lost, it's worth another $2,000 for an appeal, but it is senseless to invest $15,000 in a $50,000 lawsuit when on a statistical basis the results won't be anywhere close to 7.5 times better than they would be if an eager kid who made up in enthusiasm what he lacked in experience were given the job.[7]

The second dangerous dynamic is the tendency toward routine in large law firms. Business' strategy in almost all litigation is to browbeat and outgun its opposition. The primary justification for this approach is that 94 percent of all cases filed in court are settled before trial. Plaintiffs settle because they want money today and cannot support the expense of going to trial. At the most benign level, therefore, most business law firms resemble McDonald's restaurants; they turn out a standardized, unimaginative product that I will dub "McLaw."

At a less benign level business law firms are actually dangerous to their clients! Appellate courts frequently sustain outrageous jury awards as a penalty for not settling, and because many appellate

---

[7]Once when I was a young lawyer I was retained to represent American Brands in a lawsuit in northern West Virginia. I had recently returned from the army, and one of my fellow officers from Vietnam was an associate at Chadbourne, Parke, Whiteside, and Wolff in New York, which represented American Brands. When the case came into Chadbourne, my friend recommended me, and since American Brand's total potential exposure was about $1,000, I was given the job. It was a huge, multiparty lawsuit, and I got an enormous thrill from sending out pleadings to all of the big law firms in West Virginia with my name on them as "counsel for American Brands." I would have paid American Brands for the boost representing them gave my reputation. I got them a perfect result and forwarded a bill for $287. My friend threatened to have me committed for psychiatric care; he could never entirely understand my position that American Brands was my best client and therefore I wanted to give them good service at a fair price. He said that their level of confidence in me would have been augmented significantly if I had sent a bill for $10,000!

judges were once plaintiffs' lawyers who were on the receiving end of the dilatory motions and time-consuming discovery that McLaw firms regularly employ, they have knee-jerk, negative reactions to firepower tactics. There are, for example, a few large insurance companies who have a policy of litigating every claim unless they can get the policyholder or person suing the policyholder to settle for far less than that to which he is entitled. McLaw lawyers love these companies because they are a source of steady work, but judges know who the companies are and tune them out when they come to court because they are perennial wolf-criers.

In routine litigation where the name of the game is to soften up the other side with heavy artillery to force a favorable settlement, the McLaw approach works well; its barrage of discovery and other pretrial motions ensures that a final court judgment will not come for five years, and that encourages settlement. But in a suit that litigants cannot settle because it advances a new legal theory such as comparable worth, job security, or a new interpretation of the wage-hour law, a record full of miscellaneous, unconnected information emerging from discovery and procedural maneuvering distracts everyone from the real conflict and a concise analysis of the one, important issue. In precedent-shattering cases, the real issue is, "What should the law be?"

I once judged an important public utility case that involved interpretation of a state statute that permitted utilities to put new, higher rates into effect under bond before the public service commission had approved them. The suit arose in the late 1970s at the height of the energy crisis when utilities were raising their rates by unprecedented percentages to reflect escalating fuel costs and new environmental requirements. The case could not be settled; the lawyers for the consumer group were government-funded legal aid lawyers whose sole purpose in the case was to convince the state supreme court that the court should reinterpret the rate statute to prohibit putting rates into effect before commission approval. It was a close case: Law was on the side of the utilities, but the fireside equities were on the side of the consumers.

Two power companies filed briefs in that case, and each was represented by a major business law firm. The first brief had all the elements of a McLaw factory production. It talked about the statute, about how words should be interpreted in a common English sentence, and it cited endless precedent from other jurisdictions. Yet after reading that brief, the fireside equities were still on the side of the consumers, and the utilities came off as bloodsuckers. The lawyer who wrote that brief did not understand that the court was being asked to make a political decision and not a simple legal one.

The second brief, however, was one of the finest examples of brief writing that I have ever read. The argument began by conceding that consumers were up against hard times and that common humanity would appear to dictate a position contrary to the utilities' position. At that point, however, the brief stopped making concessions and related in a literate, entertaining, and compelling fashion the political history of the statutes that allow power companies to put rates in under bond. The primary thrust of this lawyer's argument had little to do with the West Virginia statute because our statute was patterned after a carefully crafted federal statute on the same subject. The brief explored the legislative history of the federal statute — how Congress had modified the statute over the years to achieve a balance between consumer and utility interests — and the brief emphasized that consumers had already achieved a considerable benefit through the political process because new rates were delayed automatically for three months after filing. The conclusion to which the brief led the judges was that the court could not improve the accommodation of legitimate competing interests that the legislature had crafted. It was this latter brief — with its sound presentation of the facts of how utilities and public service commissions operate and its gentle understanding of the political questions involved — that ultimately won the case for the utilities.

The story of the utility companies' briefs brings us to the third dynamic that is counterproductive to business' winning landmark cases: the way young associates in big law firms are educated and recruited.[8] A business law firm looks like a pyramid, with some aging, stately, and experienced senior partners at its apex. Immediately below them are their protégés, the middle-age partners who are usually assigned to particular departments. And below the middle-age partners, in a ratio of two or three for every partner, are the associates, with the senior associates supervising the junior ones.[9] Clients talk to partners, but associates do the client's work.

Associates in business firms are hell-bent on becoming partners, and because most of them have gotten where they are by diligent work in college that put them into good law schools, and then diligent work in law school that put them into good firms, they believe deep in their hearts that hard work will make them partners. Therefore, these young lawyers are willing to work sixty-five-hour weeks, but much of their work, for which the client cheerfully pays, is devoted to the reinvention of the wheel. For young associates, every new problem presents a new educational frontier.

Theoretically the middle-age partners supervise and guide the

---

[8]When I was a young lawyer, I couldn't find my legal backside with both hands in a hall of mirrors at high noon, even though I had gone to a good law school and clerked one summer in a big New York firm. In fact, when I opened my own one-man law office, I found that to service the clients who came to me because I dressed and talked like a lawyer, I needed to find a lawyer myself. Fortunately, there was a seventy-two-year-old solo practitioner downstairs who was very generous and taught me how to practice law.

For the last thirteen years I have been hiring lawyers right out of law school to be my personal law clerks, and although I try to find recent graduates who are smarter than I was when I was their age, my overall experience has been that they, too, have a real hall-of-mirrors problem. This circumstance is endemic. The good law schools feed their students three years of policy and theory in the best ivory tower tradition. When students graduate from law school, they then rely on six- to ten-year apprenticeships at law firms to learn the lawyer's craft. What makes my clerks surpassingly useful to me is that there are only two of us in my office and we have a relationship that approaches an Oxford tutorial. Such one-on-one supervision, however, can't and doesn't exist in major business law firms.

[9]Sullivan and Cromwell, for example, had 279 lawyers working in the firm in June 1985, of whom eighty-three were partners.

young associates. But if the ratio of associates to partners is two to one, and the partners generate their own work in addition to supervising associates, supervision tends to come after rather than before the fact. Work product is submitted to partners for approval; partners do not give detailed instructions about what to do beforehand. Associate turnover aggravates the problem of lack of experience. Only a fraction of all the associates hired by a firm will ever make partner. It's "up or out," so the fourth-, fifth-, and sixth-year associates are constantly leaving to be replaced by recent graduates. By running a revolving door large law firms guarantee that they will never have a cadre of seasoned associates who are familiar with their clients' problems.

But if we return for a moment to the public utility case that I described above, what made the winning brief so persuasive was its intimate knowledge of the history of both federal and state regulatory schemes. The brief writer was an experienced public utility lawyer who understood the industry with all its problems as well as the cold, black letter law. The result of his understanding of both the industry and the law was that the industry's business problems were brought to life as he explained how legal rules affect real-life business operations.

The large firms have devised internal systems to reduce the problem of wheel reinvention to manageable proportions. The most popular device chosen to accomplish this feat is routine — the creation of computerized forms, standard operating procedures, stock motions, and stock arguments. This, in turn, leads to the McLaw mentality with its adherence to the principle that it is better to follow undistinguished but tested techniques than to experiment with new techniques that may be either big winners or complete failures. Unfortunately, in the precedent-shattering cases, the one-size-fits-all approach is not particularly successful. In fact, much of the success of business' adversaries, the plaintiffs' bar, in the last ten years has come from a constant willingness to experiment and advance new theories. Plaintiffs' law firms are very small; many nationally known plaintiffs' lawyers practice with only two or three associates. Con-

sequently, plaintiffs' lawyers need not lobby a hide-bound bureaucracy to secure approval to try something new.

The cynosure of the McLaw mentality is exclusive lawyer control of all matters that touch on actual or potential litigation. Obviously there is some wisdom in allowing lawyers a large measure
of control within their domain. If the public affairs department
parked a sound truck in front of a judge's house to explain a case to
him it might, indeed, jeopardize a company's case in court. But
young associates who are at the base of the McLaw pyramid may
be ignorant of, and perhaps even wildly indifferent to, the nuts and
bolts of the industries they represent. Litigation lawyers work on a
brief for an automobile manufacturer one day, argue a motion for a
computer wholesaler the next, and prepare interrogatories for a
drug distributor the next. Their vision is limited, therefore, to the
closed field of legal analysis; they haven't either the training or industrial experience to relate the application of abstract legal rules to
their client's peculiar business.[10] Furthermore, business lawyers
usually do not write in an engaging fashion. Carl Sagan, who can
make astrophysics accessible to smart eighth graders, is the type of
person who should be supervising the preparation of environmental briefs; John Kenneth Galbraith would have done a great job for
Thor Power Tool; and Milton Friedman could explain the complex-
ities of rate regulation to even the stupidest appellate judge.

---

[10]There are many exceptions. For example, I remember an important case
concerning efforts by the state tax commissioner to tax interstate telephone
calls. The telephone company was defended by both its house counsel and
the largest business law firm in Charleston, whose tax lawyer spent several days at the telephone company learning about the technology of
long-distance, interstate telephone calls. The result of his extensive, self-
imposed education was that the first ten pages of the brief were a well-
written short course on how telephone calls are handled by the local company and the long-distance carrier. The technical presentation was worthy
of a good high school physics text, and it showed in a graphic manner the
physics and mechanics of the business setting in which we were to apply
the provisions of the tax statute. The case was very close, but the telephone company prevailed because of its lawyer's superbly written explanation of why all of the elements of a long-distance conversation did not
"begin and end in West Virginia," the basic requirement for a taxable
transaction under the state tax code.

Strangely enough, all of these eminent articulators (or at least younger versions who have not yet achieved national reputations and are looking for work) are probably available as consultants for about the same price that business is now paying former law review editors who just graduated from good law schools.

In general, it has been my experience that the public affairs staff does a better job of explaining the nuts and bolts of an industry than the lawyers. It has, or is able to procure, literary expertise. And its executives spend every day studying one industry with all of its industrial, scientific, and political problems. Presenting public utility rate regulation cases to a court, for example, involves explaining some complex scientific and economic matters. Many lawyers (perhaps from a sense of frustration because scientific evidence and complex accounting are mysteries to them) adopt the approach that if you can't dazzle the judges with brilliance, you can at least baffle them. Judges, unfortunately, respond negatively to bafflements. When public utility lawyers make rate regulation complex and incomprehensible to me (although I am always interested in understanding the subject), I hold for the public service commission on the theory that the commission understands the problem better than I do!

In this chapter I have dwelled on opportunities to improve business's performance at the margin within the confines of the present system. Now it is time to examine how business can improve the whole system at the margin, which is a more difficult undertaking but does not descend to the level of pure, useless speculation. In my experience systems can be neither revolutionized nor dramatically reformed, but they can be tinkered at.

Part of the problem that business is currently facing in U.S. courts is that the original rationale of the common law has been turned completely on its head. Originally, the purpose of the common law was to unify the kingdom of England; today, with fifty-three separate jurisdictions turning out their own eccentric deci-sional law, the effect of the common law is near-anarchy. Instead of unifying the United States by establishing one understandable and nationally enforceable system of laws, the competitive decisions, turf wars, and conflicting public policies of separate state court sys-tems make U.S. law inconsistent, unpredictable, and highly erratic.

And from business' perspective there is an even more sinister side of these tendencies than mere anarchy. Business is the victim of competitive efforts among the state courts to keep citizens of their own states in as favorable a position *vis-à-vis* recoveries from na-tional, nonresident corporations as the citizens of other states. Every month the American Trial Lawyers Association, which is the professional society of the plaintiffs' bar, publishes a magazine called *Trial*. In the back of that magazine are pages of advertise-ments for expert witnesses who are specialists in proving different types of torts. There are, for example, associations of experts who are concerned only with parking lot injuries and others who spe-cialize in rapes and robberies on company premises that allegedly result from negligent private security. Imaginative plaintiffs' law-yers think up new causes of action against business, and if one state court allows recovery, that recovery creates a precedent that plain-tiffs' lawyers (combined with nationally available fast-gun-for-hire experts) in other states can use to win cases there.

Obviously, it is not possible to create an entirely risk-free soci-ety; therefore, today's big question in the law is where collective responsibility for accidents ends and individual responsibility be-gins. I do not know where we should draw that line, but I do know that because of the anarchy that prevails among state jurisdictions, at the present time no line can be drawn at all. The logic of collective action[11] implies that no one state or group of states will undertake

---

[11]See M. Olson, *The Logic of Collective Action* (Cambridge, Mass.: Harvard University Press, 1971 rev. ed.).

to act responsibly in the face of irresponsibility on the part of neighboring states.[12]

Drawing a line concerning business' tort liability, then, must inevitably be done at the national level. Currently there are bills before Congress that attempt to limit different types of tort liability, particularly products liability and medical malpractice. Yet for all the reasons explored in chapter 5, the chances of these bills' passing in any form, much less a form favorable to business, are small. Ironically, the most likely place for such "legislation" to be adopted is in the Supreme Court of United States.

Although it goes against a fifty-year Supreme Court tradition, using common law principles to unify the nation is not a new idea. In fact, from 1842 to 1938 it was the rule. In *Swift v. Tyson*[13] the Supreme Court, led by Justice Story, held that when hearing nonfederal claims federal courts should apply "general federal common law." This scheme lasted until *Erie Railroad v. Tompkins*[14] in 1938, when the Court, led by Justice Brandeis, held that under the Constitution there is no such thing as "general federal common law." From that day on, federal courts hearing nonfederal claims in diversity cases were to apply the state law of the state where the claim would have been tried if it had not been brought in or removed to federal court.

Both the *Swift* and the *Erie* schemes have their deficiencies. However, what should be noted for our purposes is that the two

---

[12]The pressure for continuous expansion of the frontiers of tort law is significantly reduced when both the plaintiffs and defendants are residents of the same state. Consequently, I expect that in the next few years a host of special rules will be developed to cover tort litigation in cases that are regularly intrastate. For example, in 1985 the insurance premiums for day care centers rose as much as 1,000 percent in some areas because of increased litigation. Some day care providers closed because they could no longer provide service at an affordable price. However, because the availability of day care is a major women's issue, it is likely that state courts themselves will circumscribe the liability of day care providers. But what makes this undertaking surpassingly easy — aside from the intense political pressure from ordinary working people to keep day care providers in business — is that day care is an entirely local industry.

[13]16 U.S. (Pet.) 1 (1842).

[14]304 U.S. 64 (1938).

schemes are predicated on different visions of federalism. Justice Story saw the federal courts as a way to unify a large, diverse, and growing nation. Justice Brandeis was suspicious of this federally imposed uniformity; he saw each state as a potential laboratory for social experimentation. Under the Brandeis view, different states would adopt different laws, and through a type of Darwinian struggle, the superior laws would prevail. If the federal courts imposed uniform laws nationwide, this process of natural selection would be destroyed.

Neither Justice Story's scheme nor Justice Brandeis's scheme is appropriate for today's problems. Federal common law à la *Swift v. Tyson* does not solve the problem of chaotic state law applied in state courts, and Justice Brandeis's scheme articulated in *Erie* never contemplated today's volume of tort litigation, the diversity of state court views on the extent to which all risks should be borne by deep pockets, or the 12 to 15 million lawsuits that are now filed in U.S. courts each year. The new scheme that must emerge for this era of U.S. history will resemble neither Justice Story's nor Justice Brandeis's; the Supreme Court must unify the law of torts in the same way that it unified U.S. criminal law between 1966 and 1976.

Before the Roosevelt court of the late 1930s the U.S. Supreme Court intervened decisively in the states' regulation of economic matters, and the tools for that undertaking before 1936 are still available. Principally, those tools consist of the "commerce, " "impairment of contracts," "due process," and "equal protection" clauses of the Constitution.[15] But there is an irony here in suggesting that

---

[15]In fact, in one area of tort law, namely libel and slander, the U.S. Supreme Court has nationalized the whole area under the first amendment: Since *New York Times v. Sullivan*, 376 U.S. 254 (1963), the Supreme Court has severely circumscribed libel and slander actions and has given the states almost no latitude for eccentric local law. The reason, of course, has to do with the Court's political agenda. Libel and slander have implications for the political process, and although the profitability and continued survival of news media are at stake, the issues spill over to other questions involving the societywide distribution of wealth and power that concerns the Supreme Court. *New York Times v. Sullivan* itself arose in the context of civil rights protests in the south during the 1960s when the *New York Times* was on the side of integration while the libel plaintiffs were defending segregation.

business think about a uniform system of court-imposed, common law rules. Business executives tend to identify with the conservative side in U.S. politics, and in conservative political circles "states' rights" are taken as a matter of faith. Realistically, of course, a knee-jerk states' rights position simply works backwards from the political results desired — lower taxes, less government intrusion, fewer "liberal" solutions to social problems, and stronger traditional institutions — to a general theory that more often than not leads to those results. But to suggest to business that more stringent regulation of state courts by the U.S. Supreme Court is good for business is counterintuitive.

Once, however, some consensus about the appropriate line between social responsibility and individual responsibility is developed, the Supreme Court can draw that line and hold it.[16] The doubter need look only to the history of criminal law between 1966 and 1976 when the lower federal courts were opened up directly, through writs of habeas corpus, to enforce the Supreme Court's rulings on individual rights, civil liberties, and criminal procedure. Now that the state courts have become used to the new rules in criminal law and automatically exclude illegal evidence and demand proper police procedure, the federal courts have withdrawn from day-to-day supervision of state criminal cases to attend to other matters. But when the U.S. Supreme Court originally put the new criminal justice system into effect, the federal court system allocated the manpower and resources to make the new rules stick.

At this point we return to the problem discussed in the last chapter of judges' making policy decisions in an information vac-

---

[16]One of the few objective standards for drawing such a line in the face of militant and diverse social philosophies is the availability and practicality of insurance. The policy behind modern tort law is that many of society's risks can be spread through universal insurance purchased by business, the cost of which is passed along to everyone else in product or service prices. At the point, however, where such insurance coverage either becomes too expensive to permit continued sale of the product or service, or becomes completely unavailable, we must then conclude that individuals must bear their own risks in that area and obtain their own insurance.

uum. If we are going to argue that business needs a nationally imposed, uniform common law in the areas where it is now the victim
of competitive state court decisions, then we must figure out what
that national common law should look like. Certainly interests other
than business must be heard on the subject, and it is important that
nonbusiness positions be incorporated into any suggested program
if that program is to be taken seriously.

But where does such a program originate? The answer is that
it originates with academic lawyers, just as the whole original law
of products liability originated with academic lawyers. The process
of developing a consensus on the legitimacy of the program, however, can be expedited in the type of seminars that Gannett sponsored for discussions about the first amendment. In such an undertaking extreme caution is the watchword. Most of government and
academia is a giant talk factory; in law and the social sciences there
are no experiments and therefore no right or wrong answers. Whenever consummate egotists, such as judges, law professors, and lawyers are thrown together for discussions, most are more interested
in talking than in listening. It is unlikely that without strong leadership such groups would agree on anything, and both agreement
and a concrete program are what we need.

Consequently, if business is to educate judges and convince the
federal courts that we need national uniformity in a number of areas
of the law, the conclusions that one wants the judges to reach on
these subjects must be worked out in advance. In the Gannett seminars, the seminar leader, Professor Arthur Miller of Harvard, had
a specific agenda, and no participant in the seminar could divert the
seminar from reaching its preordained conclusions. Professor Miller
had years of experience leading first-year law students to come to
the right conclusions through their own thought processes, and he
put those skills to work for Gannett. Seminars, therefore (if we
mean business as Gannett did), are not really occasions for working
out a program; they are occasions for a well-worked-out program to
be ratified, tinkered at, and then taken home to the real world. Of
course, if one starts with a one-sided program, the seminar partici-

pants will simply come, talk with their friends, eat the seminar food, drink the seminar liquor, and enjoy themselves.

The great impediment to all of this is that business is not really a collective entity. Often different businesses are more at odds with one another than they are with forces outside business. Insurance companies, for example, want to force the automobile producers to install airbags, so they eagerly await the state court ruling that finds an automobile producer at fault for making a car without airbags. The agenda goes unprepared because no one business can afford to invest the resources necessary to do the thing alone, and different businesses' views of the proper agenda imperils cooperation among businesses. It is here that foundations like Brookings, Heritage, Aspen, and the American Enterprise Institute may play a decisive role as arbiters of different business positions as well as business versus antibusiness positions.

For example, one or more insurance companies might commission a foundation to craft model U.S. Supreme Court decisional law limiting causes of action and the type of recoveries in tort cases. The foundation could then organize seminars for federal judges, practicing lawyers, law professors, and nonlawyer academics to ratify and refine the program. Ideally, out of such an operation would come articles for magazines like *The Atlantic, The New Republic, Commentary,* and the *National Review,* which are more regularly read by judges than all the law reviews combined. And just as Gannett made some of its seminars on the first amendment into PBS television shows, the foundation could do the same with high-level discussions about unifying parts of our common law. It takes a while for such ideas to jell, but this is exactly what business does in every other area of politics: It lobbies.

Finally, it should be noted that in 1986 the Supreme Court's majority consists of very old men. If popular reports and judicial gossip can be believed, many of these men would by now have retired were it not for their fear that ideologically radical successors would be appointed by the Reagan administration. The Court, as currently constituted, therefore, is unlikely to break new ground in any direction: Both age and exhaustion eventually take their toll on even the greatest statesmen. But in the next few years the Grim Reaper will make voluntary retirement a moot question, and at that point business must try to focus the president's attention on candidates who have commercial law agendas. It is not necessary that these candidates have track records that show them in business' corner every time, but it is necessary that they have track records showing that commercial law is as important to them as church/state relations, criminal law, civil rights, and agency review. Furthermore, none of these other areas need be sacrificed to bring commercial law to the forefront because the U.S. Supreme Court, with a few minor changes in procedure, could decide twice as many cases every year as it currently decides.[17]

As it stands now, all the discussion about Supreme Court candidates centers in where they stand on abortion, civil rights, prayer in school, and a few other hot social issues. I do not mean to imply that these issues are not important, but if some litmus test on these issues must be passed, there are thousands of lawyers and hundreds of judges who can meet any such test and who also take commercial law seriously. Business will never get a 100 percent pro-business judge; such a person would not make it through the confirmation hearings. But what business can get are some judges who believe that issues such as competitive state law and costly nuisance suits are important and should be given a new look.

If one asks bright college freshmen what careers they plan to follow, often they will say that they are deciding between law and medicine. To many who are not trained in either profession, both law and medicine appear to be scientific disciplines. Such, however, is not the case. A doctor can study internal medicine all his life and specialize in ailments of the liver. Fortunately for him, all livers

---

[17]See J. Sexton, "New York University Supreme Court Project," 59 *New York University Law Review* 677 (1984).

among all races of the world (with minor individual variations) behave exactly the same. And when a patient has a severely injured
or badly diseased liver, the greatest medical specialist in the world
is limited in what he or she can do. But if a damaged liver were a
legal, instead of a medical problem, the Supreme Court of the
United States could simply declare one kidney a *de facto* liver and
cure the patient. That circumstance obviously raises a daunting
spectre of significant judicial jeopardy for business, but it also offers
endless opportunities to improve the current system. It's all a matter
of how business plays out its hand.

Index

About the Author

Justice Richard Neely is a graduate of Dartmouth College and the Yale Law School. He was elected to the West Virginia Supreme Court of Appeals in 1972, where he was Chief Justice in 1980 and 1985. Between his graduation from Yale and his election to the Supreme Court, Neely served as an Army artillery captain in Vietnam and practiced law in his own one-man office in Fairmont, West Virginia. In 1970, he served one term in the West Virginia Legislature. In addition to his judicial duties, he is professor of economics at the University of Charleston and the author of *How Courts Govern America*, *Why Courts Don't Work*, and *The Divorce Decision*.